IØ224675

BETWEEN DESERT STORM AND IRAQI FREEDOM
U.S. Army Operations in the Middle East, 1991–2001

by
Jourden Travis Moger

CENTER OF MILITARY HISTORY
UNITED STATES ARMY
WASHINGTON, D.C., 2021

CONTENTS

FIGURE

TABLE

MAPS

ILLUSTRATIONS

Front cover: Members of Task Force 1–9 wait in their Bradley
   Fighting Vehicles during Intrinsic Action 96–3, September
   1996. (*Desert Voice*)

Unless otherwise noted, all images are from the U.S. Army.

FOREWORD

The United States led military coalitions against Iraq in the 1990–1991 Persian Gulf War and the 2003 overthrow of the Saddam Hussein regime. Although these events are among the most studied in recent American military history, the U.S. operations in the Middle East between the two conflicts are much less well known. This monograph fills this gap and recounts how the U.S. Army helped deter Iraqi aggression during this period.

Between DESERT STORM *and* IRAQI FREEDOM also chronicles how the Army maintained a high tempo of operations during a decade of downsizing and consolidation. The shifting geopolitical realities after the end of the Cold War caused senior leadership to transform the Army. Its personnel numbers shrank to the lowest level since 1940, and the service reduced the number of active duty divisions from eighteen to ten. Despite these drawdowns, the potential for war in the Middle East compelled the U.S. military to maintain a modest forward presence while building the capacity to deploy troops rapidly to the region. The Army drastically cut the number of installations and increased the size of some remaining ones. It strengthened stateside infrastructure in order to move troops and equipment efficiently and quickly from U.S. garrisons to air- and seaports of embarkation. In times of crisis, the Army rushed brigades to Kuwait to serve as a deterrence force, but no fighting took place between U.S. and Iraqi ground combat units in the interwar period.

By the end of the decade, Iraq retained the ability to threaten its neighbors with conventional arms, and concerns about its illicit weapons programs persisted. To counter these twin dangers, the international community used a combination of economic sanctions and weapons inspections, while the United States and its allies applied military pressure. However, the terrorist attacks on 11 September 2001 changed America's strategic calculus. When the administration of President George W. Bush made the decision to resort to force to depose Saddam Hussein in 2003, it was able to do so thanks in part to the new power projection capabilities that the Army had developed during the interim.

Washington, D.C.   JON T. HOFFMAN
5 May 2021   Chief Historian

ACKNOWLEDGMENTS

U.S. Army records management post–Gulf War through 2001 was limited, which made finding sources for this project my biggest challenge. A search for Third Army/U.S. Army Central records yielded only documents preserved incidentally in other collections, not as a whole. The main primary source repositories for the post–Gulf War operations discussed in this monograph are the U.S. Army Center of Military History in Washington, D.C., and the U.S. Army Heritage and Education Center in Carlisle, Pennsylvania. The U.S. Air Force Historical Research Agency in Montgomery, Alabama, has numerous documents from the period related to Operation Southern Watch and Joint Task Force Southwest Asia. Command Chronologies for specific U.S. Marine Corps units involved in the operations discussed in this volume reside at the Archives Branch, Marine Corps History Division, Quantico, Virginia.

Some of the ideas in this book took shape at an excellent conference of the Society for Military History hosted by the College of Arts & Sciences and the Department of History, University of Louisville, Kentucky, 5–8 April 2018. The results of the paper I presented there became an earlier version of a portion of this study, which appeared as "The Race for Kuwait: Operation Vigilant Warrior, October–December 1994," in *Army History* 115 (Spring 2020). The Society for History in the Federal Government awarded this article the 2020 James Madison Prize.

I owe a debt of gratitude to many people who made this project possible. For their guidance and support on the development of the manuscript, I thank the members of the editorial board: Jon T. Hoffman, David W. Hogan Jr., and William S. Story. John J. Mortimer served as my graduate assistant for a year and found many of the sources used in this monograph. For their help in providing both documentation and expertise, I appreciate Christopher D. Holmes of the Joint History and Research Office at the Pentagon and David A. Dawson at U.S. Central Command. Two outside readers offered valuable advice: Brig. Gen. (Ret.) John S. Brown, the former chief of military history, and Michael W. Clauss at U.S. Army Central. Melissa K. Wiford and Pamela A. Cheney at the Army Heritage and Education Center made available many documents used in this study. Numerous colleagues read portions of this monograph and offered suggestions for improvement, including Nicholas J. Schlosser, a valuable mentor and subject matter expert throughout the project, and Jeffrey J. Seiken, who provided assistance in the early stages of my research and writing. Forrest L. Marion and other staff historians at the

Air Force Historical Research Agency answered my questions about air operations and provided relevant original documents. At the Center of Military History, Margaret J. B. McGarry edited the final draft, Michael R. Gill designed the cover and layout, and Matthew T. Boan prepared the maps. Several librarians and archivists at the Center tracked down source material and literature, one of whom deserves special recognition. James A. Tobias provided valuable research assistance on this manuscript even as he fought his own battle with terminal cancer. I dedicate this volume to his memory.

On 6 October 1994, U.S. intelligence analysts discovered clear evidence that Iraq was deploying two elite *Republican Guard* armored divisions to the Kuwaiti border. Even as he began a rapid mobilization of U.S. forces to meet the Iraqi threat, General J. H. Binford Peay III, Commander in Chief of U.S. Central Command (CINCCENT), discussed with his deputy, Marine Corps Lt. Gen. Richard I. Neal, the possibility of evacuating the small, lightly defended U.S. base, Camp Doha, located west of Kuwait City.

The problem was time. Was there time to evacuate the approximately 500 Army personnel and 1,200 civilians on the post when the Iraqi army was only a few hours away? If the Iraqis were to cross the border, should the Army garrison abandon, move, or destroy all the Abrams tanks, Bradley fighting vehicles, and howitzers stored at Camp Doha? How long could the Kuwaiti military with its four brigades hold off Iraq's two armored divisions? And perhaps the most important question on General

General Peay

General Neal

(U.S. Marine Corps)

Peay's mind: Was there time to rush enough forces into theater to stop the Iraqi *Republican Guard* from overrunning Kuwait as they had in August 1990?

In February 1991, the United States and its allies had won a lopsided victory over Iraq in the Gulf War. It took just six weeks of air attacks and a hundred hours of ground combat to overwhelm the Iraqi army—the fourth-largest army in the world—and push it out of Kuwait. Despite the decisive outcome, this war did not remove Iraqi President Saddam Hussein from power. Nor did it eliminate his ability to threaten neighboring countries and vital U.S. interests in the region, especially the free flow of oil.[1] During the subsequent decade, the U.S. Army combined its forward presence in Kuwait with a rapid deployment of ground forces in times of escalating crisis. In this way, the Army, as part of a larger coalition and joint effort, played an important role in deterrence operations in Southwest Asia until the decision to launch a second and more controversial war against Iraq in 2003.[2]

---

1. On the free flow of oil as a vital U.S. national interest, see William J. Perry, *Public Statements of William J. Perry Secretary of Defense, 1996–97*, vol. 3 (Washington, DC: Historical Office, Office of the Secretary of Defense, n.d.), 1533; [William] Anthony [K.] Lake, "Confronting Backlash States," *Foreign Affairs* 73, no. 2 (Mar-Apr 1994): 47–48.
2. Deterrence is "the prevention of action by the existence of a credible threat of unacceptable counteraction and/or belief that the cost of action outweighs the perceived benefits." A related term, contain, refers to "a tactical mission task that requires the commander to stop, hold, or surround enemy forces or to cause them to center their activity on a given front and prevent them from withdrawing any part of their forces for use elsewhere." Army Doctrine Reference Publication 1–02, *Terms and Military Symbols* (Washington, DC: Army Publishing Directorate, Headquarters, Department of the Army, 16 Nov 2016), 1-21, 1-29.

IRAQ—1920s THROUGH 1980s

Iraq's strategic significance lies in its location and natural resources. Assembled from three provinces of the former Ottoman Empire after World War I, the modern state of Iraq came into being in 1920 as a British mandate. In 1932, the mandate ended. Iraq became an independent state, still closely tied to Britain, and a member of the League of Nations.[3] The new nation encompassed the lands of ancient Mesopotamia, abutting the northern edge of the Arabian Peninsula. Before the discovery of oil in 1927, the area's strategic significance derived principally from geography, as Iraq lay across ancient east-west trade routes.[4] Even in the twentieth century, its location made Iraq coveted real estate. From 1903 until 1940, Germany endeavored to expand its overseas influence by connecting itself to the Persian Gulf via the Berlin-Baghdad Railway.

Iraq's political and physical geography exacerbated rivalries with its neighbors, especially Iran and Kuwait. Iran borders Iraq on the east; Kuwait and Saudi Arabia lie to the south; Jordan and Syria are to the west; and Turkey is to the north. The Arabian and Syrian Deserts extend into the arid south and west of the country. Rugged mountains border Iran and Turkey in the far north. A fertile plain, encompassing the Tigris and Euphrates River Valleys, stretches from the far northwest near Syria to the Persian Gulf in the extreme southeast. (*See Map 1.*) Iraq has limited access to the sea. The Khawr Abd Allah, an estuary, connects the northernmost part of the gulf with Iraq's only deep-water port, Umm Qasr. Ships sailing to and from this seaport must pass Kuwait's Al Warbah and Bubiyan Islands. Al Basrah, Iraq's other major port city, lies 110 kilometers up the strategically located Shatt al Arab, which flows from the confluence of the Tigris and Euphrates, 83 kilometers upstream from Al Basrah, and divides Iran and Iraq at the southernmost part of their common border.[5] (*See Map 2.*) Iraq's largest cities, all with populations

---

3. In exchange for independence, Iraq signed a mutual defense treaty with the United Kingdom, and allowed British air bases to remain at Habbaniyah near Baghdad and Shaibah near Al Basrah. Britain also retained control of the Iraqi part of the Berlin-Baghdad Railway as well as the pipeline network from the Kirkuk oil fields to Tripoli and Haifa. T. H. Vail Motter, *The Persian Corridor and Aid to Russia*, United States Army in World War II (1952; Washington, DC: U.S. Army Center of Military History, 2000), 8.

4. Iraq's petroleum industry began with the discovery of oil at Baba Gurgur (literally, "Father of Fire") near the city of Kirkuk on 15 October 1927. Daniel Yergin, *The Prize: The Epic Quest for Oil, Money, and Power* (New York: Free Press, 2009), 187–88.

5. Phebe Marr, *The Modern History of Iraq*, 3rd ed. (Boulder, CO: Westview Press, 2012), 11. Note: *Shatt al Arab* means "the Arab stream."

Berlin-Baghdad Railway, ca. 1900–1910
(Library of Congress)

more than one million today, are located along navigable rivers: Baghdad and Mosul on the Tigris and Al Basrah on the Shatt al Arab. Access to the sea, vitally important for Iraq's oil industry, was a major factor in the wars it fought in the late twentieth century.

The new Iraqi state brought together diverse ethnic and religious groups. A Shi'a Muslim majority was concentrated in the south, and a Sunni Muslim minority in the central and northern areas.[6] Both the Ottomans and the British elevated the country's Sunni minority to positions of power—the Ottomans because they were coreligionists and the British to keep the status quo. Sunnis continued to dominate the political sphere until the U.S.–led invasion of Iraq in 2003. A small number of Arab Christians (Chaldean Catholics) and Yazidis rounded out all but a tiny fragment of the religious demographic. Ethnically, Iraq has an Arab majority of Shi'a, Sunnis, and Christians, comprising roughly 75 to 80 percent of the population. The predominantly Sunni Kurds, who live mostly in northern Iraq, make up 15 to 20 percent of the population. Turkmen, Assyrians, and other ethnic minorities account for around 5 percent. For much of its independent history, Iraq's population existed in an uneasy national unity, albeit one in which internal rivalries were never entirely suppressed.

Cross-border ethnic and religious demographics complicated the geopolitical situation in the Middle East, increased security challenges, and limited Iraq's ability to maintain a unified national identity. Across Iraq's northern border, Turkey had its own Kurdish minority with ties to Iraqi Kurds. To the east, Iran also had a Kurdish minority, but most of its

---

6. The noun *Shi'a* means "party of Ali" and designates both the branch of Islam and its adherents. It is also an adjective, as in "Shi'a Islam."

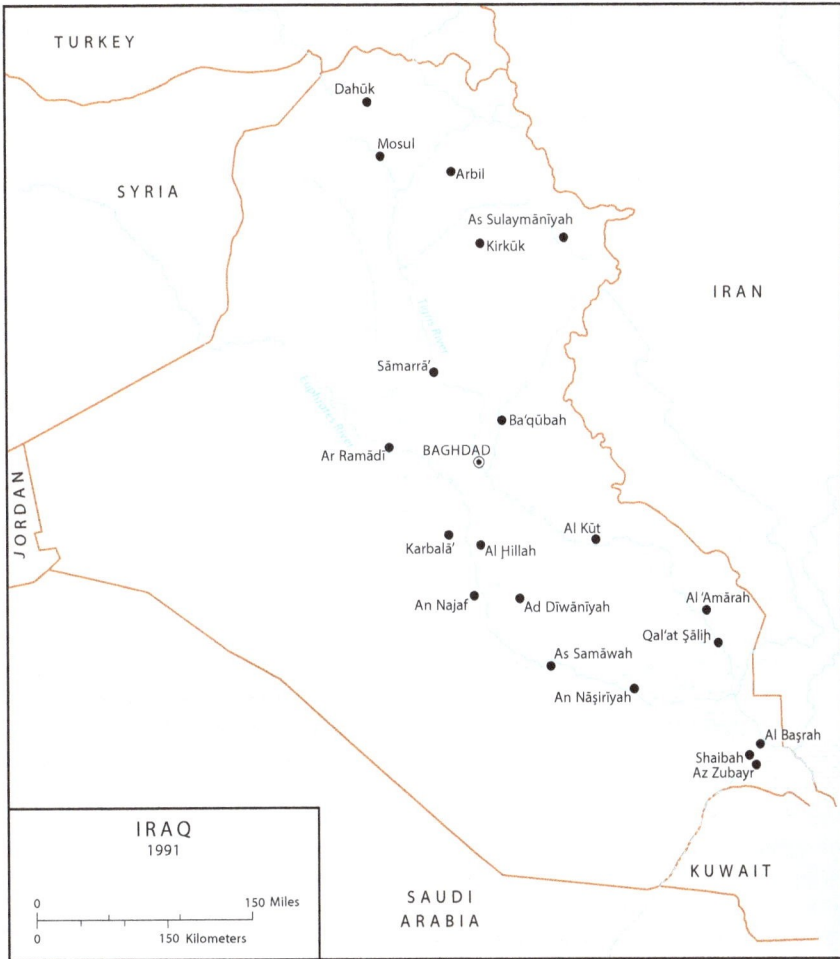

Map labels:

TURKEY

SYRIA

Dahūk

Mosul

●Arbil

As Sulaymānīyah

●Kirkūk

IRAN

Sāmarrā'●

●Ba'qūbah

Ar Ramādī●   BAGHDAD ◉

JORDAN

Al Kūt

Karbalā'   ●Al Ḩillah

An Najaf   ●Ad Dīwānīyah

Al 'Amārah

Qal'at Şāliḩ●

As Samāwah

An Nāşirīyah

Al Başrah

Shaibah●
Az Zubayr●

IRAQ
1991

0   150 Miles
0   150 Kilometers

KUWAIT

SAUDI
ARABIA

Map 1

population remained ethnically and linguistically Persian. The majority of Iranians adhered to the Shi'a branch of Islam. Historic Arab-Persian, Arab-Kurdish, and Sunni-Shi'a divides served as fault lines along which tensions erupted repeatedly. Iraq's mostly Sunni leadership guarded against Iran's attempts to incite rebellion among Iraqi Shi'a and Kurds. Similarly, Turkey feared that Iraqi Kurds would support their Turkish cousins' struggles against Ankara. Such deep-seated rivalries created internal and external security challenges for Iraq and its neighbors and complicated U.S. and Western diplomatic efforts in the region.

During World War II, the British controlled Iraq and Iran, which were pivotal to the Allies' defense of the Middle East. Before the United States entered the war, Britain reversed a pro-Nazi coup in Baghdad by defeating Iraqi ground troops and a contingent of the German *Luftwaffe* during a month-long operation in May 1941. This action, along with a

15

IRAQ'S ACCESS TO THE GULF
1991

0   20
Miles

Al Başrah

Shatt al Arab

Khorramshahr

IRAN

Az Zubayr

Abadan

IRAQ

Safwān

Al Faw
Peninsula

Umm Qaşr

Al Warbah

Khawr Abd Allah

Ar Rawḍatayn

Būbiyān

KUWAIT

PERSIAN GULF

KUWAIT BAY

Maskān

Az Zawr   Faylakah

Camp
Doha

KUWAIT

'Awhah

Al Jahrah

As Sālimīyah

Al Aḥmadī   Al Fuḥ ayḥ īl

Kubbar

Map 2

successful Allied campaign against Vichy French Syria and Lebanon, deprived Adolf Hitler of a foothold in the oil-rich region. After Germany attacked the Soviet Union in June 1941, British and Soviet troops invaded Iran to secure its oil facilities, ports, and roads (*Map 3*). The U.S. Army deployed some 30,000 troops in support of this effort, beginning in November 1941 and lasting four years.[7] These soldiers fell under what eventually would be called the Persian Gulf Command, whose mission was to supply the Soviet Union with equipment, fuel, ammunition, food, and medical supplies as part of the wartime lend-lease program.[8] The main American-led missions were in Iran, where U.S. troops improved and ran the Iranian State Railway and two major seaports served by it: Khorramshahr on the Shatt al Arab and Bandar Shahpur (now Bandar Emam) at the northern end of the Persian Gulf.

Following World War II, Cold War tensions and pan-Arab nationalism fueled instability throughout the Middle East. Political division, combined with the lack of an effective internal security apparatus, made the Iraqi government vulnerable to repeated military coups. In July 1958, an Iraqi army general named Abd al-Karim Qasim led a coup that deposed King Faisal II. Rebels executed the former monarch along with several other members of Iraq's royal family. Qasim became the prime minister and minister of defense in a new Republic of Iraq. The following decade was characterized by instability, military dictatorship, and a shift from a British-oriented foreign policy to a Soviet-aligned one. After the 1958 coup, Iraq began buying arms from the Soviet Union instead of its traditional Western suppliers, Great Britain and the United States, which had always set limits on arms sales to Iraq. For the first time since the Iraqi army's establishment in 1921, Iraq could purchase military equipment from its new benefactors without restrictions.[9] In 1968, the Baath Party seized power under the leadership of Ahmad Hasan al-Bakr and his cousin and protégé Saddam Hussein. The two moved quickly and ruthlessly to consolidate their authority, eliminate rivals, neutralize the military, and build a single-party system with an elaborate security apparatus.

The new Iraqi government faced challenges from within and without. In 1969, neighboring Iran, then a U.S. ally, pushed its claim to share the Shatt al Arab, which connects both the Iraqi port city of Al Basrah and the Iranian port city of Abadan to the Persian Gulf. Iran began piloting its own ships down the river and stopped paying transit fees to Iraq. When Iraq retaliated, Iran began supplying aid to Iraqi Kurds seeking to break away from Baghdad's control. Through a covert Central Intelligence

---

7. Motter, *Persian Corridor*, 7, 28. "Peak assigned U.S. military strength came in February 1944 with 29,691 officers and men." Ibid., 241n3.
8. *An Act Further to Promote the Defense of the United States, and For Other Purposes*, PL 77–11, 77th Congress (Cong.), 1st session (sess.), 11 Mar 1941, ch. 11.
9. Pesach Malovany, *Wars of Modern Babylon: A History of the Iraqi Army from 1921 to 2003* (Lexington: University of Kentucky Press, 2018), 25.

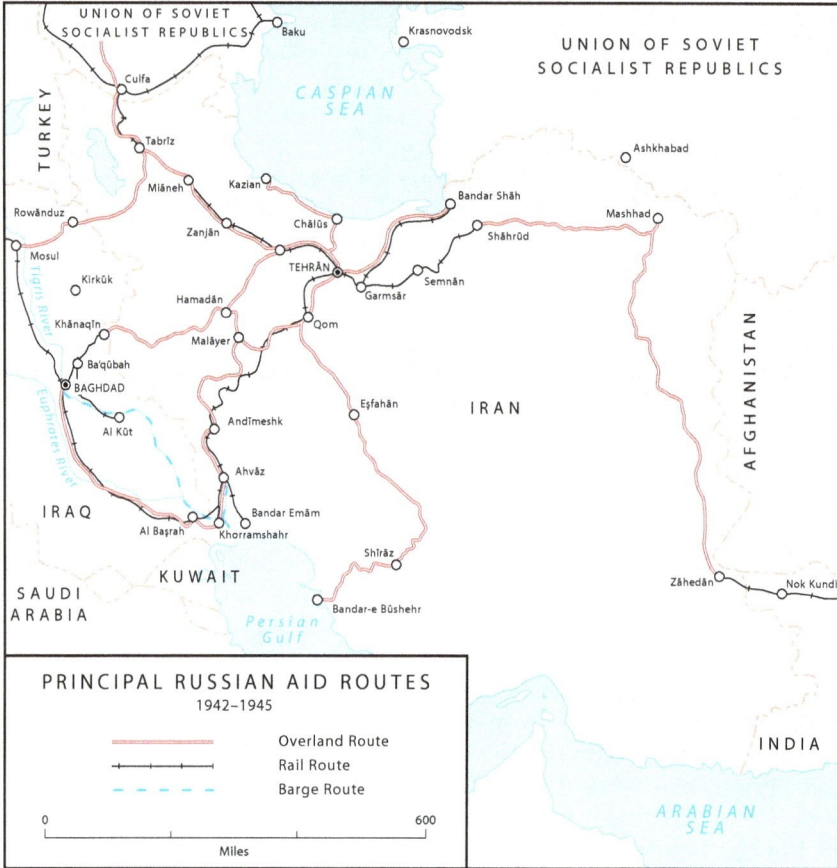

Map 3

Agency (CIA) program, the United States also began providing aid to the Kurds in 1971. The situation deteriorated until the Kurds, with direct military support from Iran, fought the Iraqi military to a stalemate in a 1974–1975 war. The agreement that ended the war gave Iran most of what it wanted, including shared rights to the Shatt al Arab, but it left the Kurdish national movement in disarray and forced its leaders and most of its guerrilla fighters (known as the *Peshmerga*, literally "those who would face death") into exile. Both Iraq and Iran improved their positions at the expense of the Kurds.

Despite the costs of the 1974–1975 war, Iraq prospered in the 1970s. Much of the country's wealth came from oil: Iraq owned 10 percent of the world's oil reserves, second only to Saudi Arabia, which had a quarter. In the 1973 Yom Kippur War, Israel defeated a coalition of Arab states, including Iraq. The Organization of Arab Petroleum Exporting Countries then embargoed nations that had supported Israel. The resulting rise in oil prices filled the coffers of oil-producing nations. Iraq used its increased revenue to build its military, improve infrastructure

Shatt al Arab in the city of Al Basrah, Iraq
(Wikimedia Commons)

including government-owned industries, and create a welfare state that offered free education and healthcare services. Living standards improved, especially for poorer Iraqis. Some of Iraq's new wealth went to covert weapons programs. In 1974, the Baath regime began a secret program, directed by Saddam Hussein, to develop chemical, biological, and nuclear weapons. Although its weapons of mass destruction (WMD) program never produced a nuclear weapon, Iraq used chemical weapons on numerous occasions and with lethal effect in years to come, against both Iran and Iraqi Kurds.

THE IRAN-IRAQ WAR AND EXPANDING U.S. INVOLVEMENT IN THE MIDDLE EAST

The 1979 Egypt-Israel Peace Treaty had the potential to herald an era of peace in the Middle East, but tensions soon spiked because of the long-standing Arab-Persian rivalry. Earlier the same year, Saddam Hussein expelled Iranian Shi'a religious leader Ayatollah Ruhollah Khomeini from Iraq, where he had been living in exile. The following year, both men would assume power in Iraq and Iran respectively, setting the stage for a violent confrontation between their two nations.

The political upheaval of 1979 fundamentally reshaped the dynamics of power in both Tehran and Baghdad. After a year of protests and violence against authorities led by antigovernment Islamists, Shah Mohammed Reza Pahlavi left Iran on 16 January 1979, suffering from terminal cancer. The shah hoped that his departure would be a temporary measure to calm the country's civil unrest, but he would never return. Two weeks later, on 1 February, Khomeini arrived in Tehran to a hero's welcome. In March, the Iranian people approved a referendum to replace the monarchy with an Islamic Republic, paving the way for Khomeini to become the new Iranian head of state that fall. In Baghdad, by contrast, the transition of power was less contested. Saddam Hussein, who had served as vice president of Iraq for eleven years, forced Ahmad Hasan al-Bakr to retire, succeeding him as president of Iraq in July. After Saddam assumed supreme power, violence in Iraq was limited to his suppression—and, in some cases, exile or execution—of dissident clerics and his bloody purge of the Baath Party's top leadership, amid rumors of a Syrian-backed plot to topple the Iraqi regime.[10]

The new Iraqi leader feared that the fundamentalist Shi'a Iranian Revolution would spill over the border, incite Iraq's Shi'a majority, and threaten the Baath Party's secular regime. At the same time, Iran seemed a vulnerable target; it had isolated itself from the West and purged its U.S.-trained military officer corps. Saddam decided to invade Iran in September 1980 with the goals of exerting control over the entire Shatt al Arab, annexing oil-rich Khuzestan Province, and perhaps obtaining three disputed islands in the Strait of Hormuz, which connects the Persian Gulf and the Indian Ocean. The strategic significance of these islands lay

---

10. Charles Tripp, *A History of Iraq*, 3rd ed. (Cambridge, UK: Cambridge University Press, 2007), 212–14.

in the fact that one-fifth of the world's oil exports passed through the twenty-mile strait every day.[11]

After initial battlefield successes, Iraq failed to consolidate its gains, and the war devolved into a stalemate. By 1982, Iran had recovered its lost territory and began advancing into Iraq, threatening Al Basrah. In February 1984, as the ground war stalled, Iraq began targeting its adversary's civilian population centers with Scud missiles and bombing raids, prompting retaliatory air and artillery strikes by Iran in what was known unofficially as the War of the Cities.[12] After a few months, the new strategy brought diminishing returns for both sides. Iraq, armed with newly acquired French fighter-bombers and antiship missiles, shifted its focus to Iran's oil-dependent economy.

Instability in the Middle East motivated U.S. leaders to strengthen military command structures for the region. On 1 January 1983, the newly activated U.S. Central Command (CENTCOM), headquartered in Tampa, Florida, replaced the Rapid Deployment Joint Task Force, which the United States had created in March 1980 after the Iranian Revolution and the Soviet invasion of Afghanistan.[13] On 1 December 1982, the Army reactivated the Third United States Army (Third Army) headquarters at Fort McPherson, Georgia.[14] A month later, it assumed the role of CENTCOM's Army component. The creation of these two headquarters proved timely: soon afterward, the conflict between Baghdad and Tehran spilled into the waters of the Persian Gulf, threatening the free flow of oil.

U.S. involvement in the Iran-Iraq War increased during what was known as the Tanker War phase of the conflict, which began in March 1984. First, Iraq attacked tankers transporting Iranian oil. Iran followed suit, attacking Arab oil tankers in the Persian Gulf. To counter the threat to shipping, the United States provided Airborne Warning and Control System (AWACS) support to Saudi Arabia. With real-time intelligence gathered by American aircraft, the Royal Saudi Air Force enforced a no-fly zone over the western Gulf, while allied warships from Britain, France, and America increased their patrolling of the seas. Meanwhile, even though the United States had imposed an arms embargo on Iran in 1979, in 1985 the Ronald W. Reagan administration began covertly supplying arms to the Islamic Republic through Israeli intermediaries in exchange for Iranian assistance in the release of U.S. hostages in Lebanon. The administration then illegally funneled profits from its clandestine arms sales to paramilitary guerrilla groups, known as Contras, who

---

11. David B. Crist, *The Twilight War: The Secret History of America's Thirty-Year Conflict with Iran* (New York: Penguin, 2012), 1.

12. Pierre Razoux, *The Iran-Iraq War*, trans. Nicholas Elliott (Cambridge, MA: Belknap Harvard, 2015), 302–4.

13. Jay E. Hines, "From Desert One to Southern Watch: The Evolution of U.S. Central Command," *Joint Forces Quarterly* (Spring 2000), 42–44.

14. PO 129–2, HQ U.S. Army Forces Cmd, 15 Sep 1982, Historians Files, U.S. Army Center of Military History, Washington, DC (hereinafter CMH).

opposed the leftist Nicaraguan government. This scandal-provoking arrangement later became known as the Iran-Contra affair.

During a renewed ground offensive in early 1986, Iran captured Iraq's Al Faw peninsula, further restricting Iraq's access to the Gulf and threatening Al Basrah from the south. This surprise victory worried Kuwait and Saudi Arabia, and they increased their aid to Iraq. Then, three years into the Tanker War, the conflict took a deadly turn for the United States. On 17 May 1987, an Iraqi pilot, flying a Dassault Mirage F–1, fired two Exocet antiship missiles at the frigate USS *Stark*. Both hit their target, severely damaging the ship, killing thirty-seven American sailors, and wounding twenty-one others. Iraq quickly apologized, claiming the targeting of the *Stark* was an accident, and eventually paid compensation.

As the Tanker War escalated, the United States reflagged eleven Kuwaiti ships and began escorting them through the treacherous waters of the Persian Gulf in an operation called EARNEST WILL. Although the escort activities proved a success overall, they began badly. During the first escort mission on 24 July 1987, the reflagged tanker MV *Bridgeton* struck an underwater mine west of Iran's Jazireh-ye Farsi, an island in the middle of the Gulf. The explosion caused extensive damage and prompted the rapid deployment of U.S. minesweeping helicopters and ships to the region.

As the war entered its final year, civilians found themselves increasingly in the belligerents' crosshairs. A new phase of the war, dubbed the War of the Capitals, played out in early 1988 while both sides depleted their missiles. The Iranians then attacked northern Iraq and seized one of two major electricity-generating dams. During a counterattack, Saddam ordered the gassing of the Kurdish town of Halabjah to punish people whom he believed were helping the Iranians. Napalm and poison gas killed 3,000 to 5,000 Kurdish civilians and wounded another 10,000. This infamous "Halabjah Massacre" brought the Iranian offensive to a halt and would later provide grounds for Saddam Hussein's death sentence during his 2004 trial.[15]

Saddam Hussein
(Department of Defense)

---

15. Razoux, *Iran-Iraq War*, 438.

With the strongest Iranian forces tied down in the north, Saddam attacked in the south. On the first day of the Islamic holy month of Ramadan, 17 April 1988, the Iraqi army, led by *Republican Guard* units, surprised an outnumbered and outmatched Iranian force, killing 5,000 and capturing twice that number. The following day, the Iraqi army wrested the Al Faw peninsula from Iranian control.

In an unrelated action on 18 April, U.S. warships and aircraft destroyed two Iranian oil platforms, sank one of four Iranian frigates, and severely damaged another. Code-named PRAYING MANTIS, this maritime operation was retaliation for an Iranian mine that nearly had sunk the frigate USS *Samuel B. Roberts* four days earlier in the Persian Gulf.[16] Fighting Iraq and the United States simultaneously weakened the Iranian will to continue the war.[17]

The war's endgame played out in the late spring and summer of 1988. Iraq won unqualified victories in a series of four battles along the Iran-Iraq border from May to July. In each contest, Iran suffered high casualties and lost territory, leaving the Iranian military a spent force with neither the will nor the ability to continue fighting. For Iran, another severe blow came on 3 July 1988, when the USS *Vincennes* shot down Iran Air Flight 655, mistaking the commercial airliner for a hostile fighter jet and killing all 290 civilians aboard. Tehran saw the attack as a deliberate escalation of American involvement in the war. Coming on the heels of a series of battlefield setbacks, the downing of a civilian aircraft by an American warship gave Iran a justification

USS *Samuel B. Roberts* (FFG-58) in dry dock for repairs after striking an Iranian mine in the Persian Gulf on 14 April 1988

(National Archives)

16. Crist, *Twilight War*, 338–57; Craig L. Symonds, *Decision at Sea: Five Naval Battles that Shaped American History* (Oxford: Oxford University Press, 2005), 265–341.
17. Razoux, *Iran-Iraq War*, 449.

for accepting the United Nations (UN) cease-fire proposal without admitting defeat.[18] After eight grueling years of combat, a cease-fire took effect on 20 August 1988. The conflict ended roughly where it had begun, with neither side gaining significant territory.

The high cost of the Iran-Iraq War, in human and financial terms, laid the groundwork for Iraq's invasion of the small, oil-rich emirate of Kuwait. Baghdad used its high number of war dead as moral leverage to argue that other Arab countries should provide debt relief, because Iraqis had paid in blood to protect them from the Persian threat.[19] By war's end, Iraq had spent virtually all of its $35 billion reserves.[20] It owed $80 billion, an amount equivalent to 150 percent of its gross domestic product and roughly one and a half times the nation's annual income.[21] Due in part to infrastructure damage, estimated at $90 billion, Iraq was unable to pay these debts. Baghdad also accused Kuwait and the United Arab Emirates of pumping more oil than their allowed quotas set by OPEC (Organization of the Petroleum Exporting Countries). Overproduction helped depress the price of oil, making it even more difficult for Iraq to meet its war-related obligations. In July 1990, Saddam Hussein threatened to punish any country that pumped excess oil, claiming "the oil quota violators have stabbed Iraq with a poison dagger."[22] He demanded that Kuwait forgive Iraqi war debt and provide additional aid. Further, he accused Kuwait of stealing oil from Iraq's Rumaylah oil field by means of slant drilling and demanded compensation.

Iraq and Kuwait also had a longstanding dispute about their mutual border. Kuwait had been under formal British protection from 1899 until 1961, when it gained its independence. Almost immediately after the announcement of Kuwaiti self-rule, Baghdad laid claim to the emirate, arguing that Kuwait remained an integral part of Iraq because it had once belonged to the Ottoman province of Basra (*Map 4*). The British deployed troops to protect Kuwaiti sovereignty. Iraq formally recognized Kuwait's independence in 1963. However, territorial disputes did not end there. In 1973, the Iraqi military briefly attacked and occupied the small border post of Samita in northeastern Kuwait in an unsuccessful attempt to coerce the emirate into relinquishing control of Al Warbah and Bubiyan Islands.[23] After the Iran-Iraq War, Saddam renewed Iraq's claim to all of Kuwait. Even as he was involved in ongoing bilateral negotiations over his concerns, he moved more than 100,000 troops toward the Kuwaiti border.

---

18. Crist, *Twilight War*, 371. For the original letter, see "Text of Iranian Letter to the UN," *New York Times*, 19 Jul 1988.
19. Razoux, *Iran-Iraq War*, 470, 569. Razoux estimated the total Iraqi war dead at 350,000, of which 125,000 were Iraqi military personnel killed in action.
20. Marr, *Modern History of Iraq*, 202.
21. Joseph C. Wilson, *The Politics of Truth: Inside the Lies that Led to the War and Betrayed My Wife's CIA Identity: A Diplomat's Memoir* (New York: Carroll & Graf, 2004), 97.
22. Laurie Collier Hillstrom, ed., *The War in the Persian Gulf: Almanac* (Farmington Hills, MI: Thomason Gale, 2004), 20.
23. Juan de Onis, "Baghdad's Troops Pull Out—2 Islands are at Issue," *New York Times*, 5 Apr 1973.

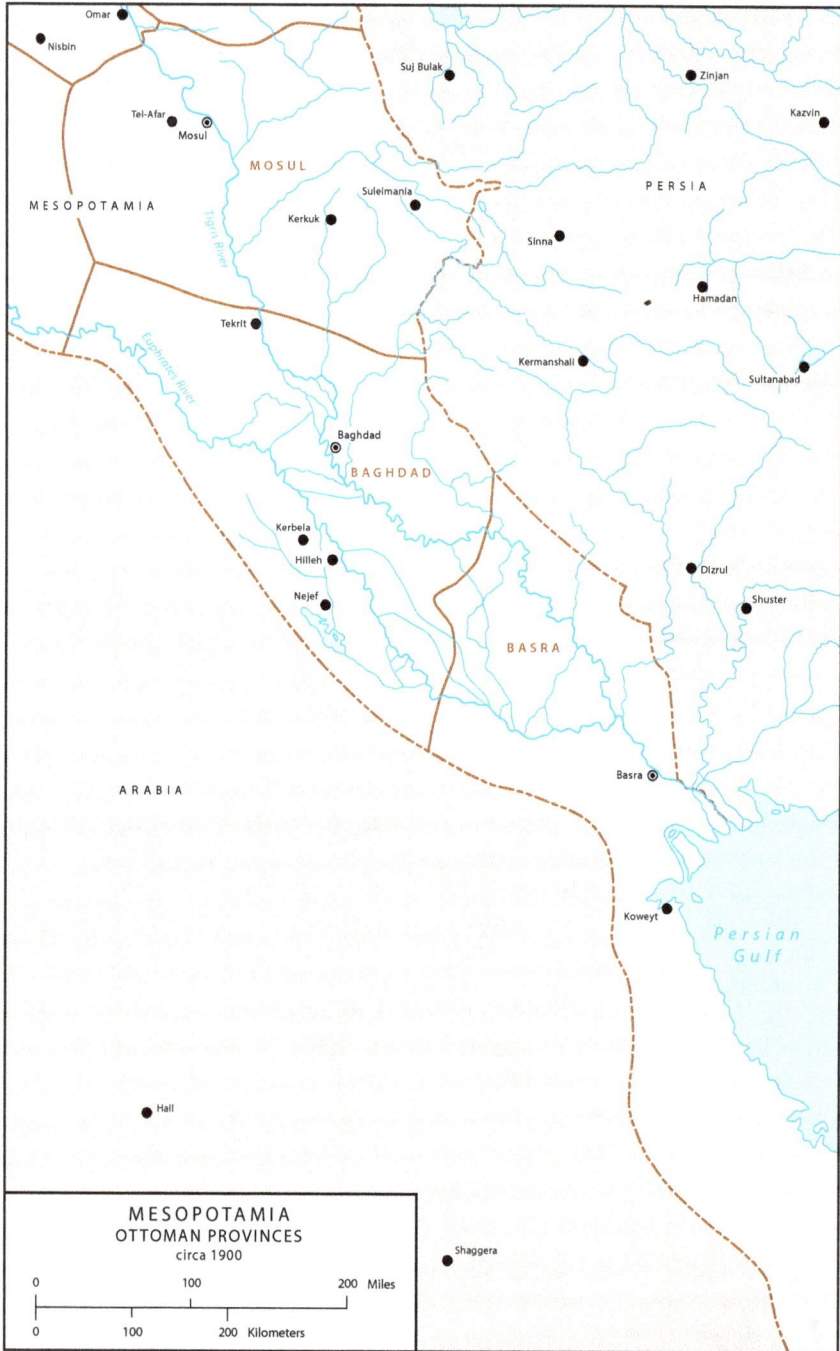

Omar
Nisbin
Tel-Afar
Mosul
Suj Bulak
Zinjan
Kazvin

MOSUL

MESOPOTAMIA

Suleimania
Kerkuk

PERSIA

Sinna

Hamadan

Tekrit

Kermanshali

Sultanabad

Baghdad

BAGHDAD

Kerbela
Hilleh
Nejef

Dizrul

Shuster

BASRA

Basra

ARABIA

Koweyt

Persian Gulf

Hail

MESOPOTAMIA
OTTOMAN PROVINCES
circa 1900

| 0 | 100 | 200 Miles |

| 0 | 100 | 200 Kilometers |

Shaggera

Tigris River

Euphrates River

Map 4

In November 1988, General H. Norman Schwarzkopf Jr. took command of CENTCOM. (*See Appendix A.*) Serving during the twilight of the Cold War, he had the foresight to revise his primary war plan, which imagined a Soviet invasion of Iran, to prepare instead for a possible Iraqi invasion of Kuwait and Saudi Arabia. From 23 to 28 July 1990, CENTCOM war-gamed the plan in Exercise INTERNAL LOOK 90, which readied Schwarzkopf's staff and subordinate commands for the approaching conflict. The preparations proved both prescient and timely.

In the predawn hours of 2 August 1990, three heavy divisions of the Iraqi army's *Republican Guard* rumbled across the Kuwaiti border and quickly overran the emirate's small, unsuspecting military. The emir, Sheikh Jaber, and the crown prince, Sheikh Saad, had barely enough warning to escape to neighboring Saudi Arabia. By midmorning, just seven hours after the attack began, the capital, Kuwait City, was in Iraqi hands. Within three days, Iraq occupied the entire country. The UN Security Council immediately condemned Iraqi aggression and demanded the withdrawal of Iraqi military forces from Kuwait. Four days later, the UN imposed a comprehensive trade embargo on Iraq, including weapons and other military equipment but excluding medical supplies and food.[24] That same day, the Saudi Arabian monarch, King Fahd, approved the deployment of coalition forces to defend his kingdom. Two days later, on 8 August, U.S. President George H. W. Bush announced Operation DESERT SHIELD as the lead elements of the 2d Brigade, 82d Airborne Division, and key units of the U.S. Air Force were arriving in Saudi Arabia to assist in protecting the kingdom. In response to the news of this intervention, Saddam formally annexed Kuwait, giving Iraq control of a fifth of the world's oil reserves. The occupying Iraqi troops looted Kuwait's wealth, mistreated civilians, and carried out political executions. Despite harsh sanctions designed to pressure Iraq to withdraw from Kuwait, Saddam Hussein remained intransigent. On 29 November 1990, the UN authorized the use of force to end the Iraqi occupation and set 15 January 1991 as the deadline for Iraq to withdraw.

Even before the UN ultimatum, President Bush had assembled a multinational force to protect Saudi Arabia and prepare for war in case Saddam refused to leave Kuwait. In the face of a real threat to

---

24. United Nations (UN) Security Council, Resolution 661, The Situation Between Iraq and Kuwait, S/RES/661, 6 Aug 1990, http://unscr.com/en/resolutions/doc/661.

their sovereignty, the Saudis had overcome their antipathy to having foreign troops on their soil, which Muslims considered sacred. General Schwarzkopf led the multinational force, which eventually comprised 700,000 troops from twenty-eight countries.[25]

The burden of preparing for land warfare fell to Lt. Gen. John J. Yeosock, commander of the Third Army. This unit had three distinct functions: (1) a field army headquarters, directing army corps and echelons above corps units (e.g., engineers, military police, civil affairs, and so on); (2) a theater army headquarters, in charge of overall logistic and service support; and (3) a service component headquarters, responsible for all U.S. Army forces in theater, excluding operational command for certain special operations forces.[26] As CENTCOM's Army component command, the Third Army was also known as U.S. Army Central (ARCENT), which made it a logical choice for the land component command headquarters as well.[27] However, General Yeosock would not command the land component. Instead, General Schwarzkopf, as

General Schwarzkopf

General Yeosock

25. Frank N. Schubert and Theresa L. Kraus, eds., *The Whirlwind War: The United States Army in Operations Desert Shield and Desert Storm* (Washington, DC: U.S. Army Center of Military History, 1994), 130.

26. Richard M. Swain, *"Lucky War": Third Army in Desert Storm* (Fort Leavenworth, KS: U.S. Army Command and General Staff College Press, 1994), 25; John J. Yeosock, "H+100: An Army Comes of Age in the Persian Gulf," *ARMY Magazine* 41, no. 10 (Oct 1991): 47–50.

27. Yeosock, "H+100," 46.

the combatant commander, would serve in this position, overseeing the overall ground forces for the looming war.

The Third Army eventually commanded two army corps. Over a two-month period in the fall of 1990, the XVIII Airborne Corps deployed from the continental United States with an airborne division, an air assault division, two heavy divisions, an armored cavalry regiment, and attached combat support and combat service support units. The French sent a light armored division to augment the XVIII Airborne Corps. In November, President Bush ordered a second army corps to Saudi Arabia. The Army's VII Corps left Germany with its two armored divisions plus one armored cavalry regiment. An additional U.S.-based mechanized infantry division augmented the corps in the theater, as did a British armored division. During Operation DESERT SHIELD, in defense of Saudi Arabia, the Third Army's forces swelled to 300,000 troops and its headquarters staff increased from roughly 300 at the start of the operation to about 1,000.[28] These additional forces allowed the Third Army to plan its ambitious and ultimately successful flanking maneuver in the desert west of Kuwait. The U.S. Navy, Marine Corps, and Air Force also built up significant forces in the region to support the operation, as did the coalition's Arab militaries.

After the UN withdrawal deadline passed in January 1991, Operation DESERT SHIELD became DESERT STORM. Yeosock understood that the mission was "to free Kuwait from Iraqi control and to destroy Iraqi offensive military capability while minimizing casualties."[29] Saddam wanted to draw the coalition into a bloody war of attrition, which he predicted would be the "Mother of All Battles."[30] He assumed that the Americans would give up as soon as casualties began to mount. In an attempt to drive a wedge between Arab and non-Arab states within the coalition, he fired scores of Scud missiles at Israel, hoping the attacks would draw the Israelis into the war. Saddam also attacked Saudi Arabia with Scuds. A five-week coalition air campaign, which began on 17 January 1991, was followed by a hundred-hour ground war. In just four days of ground fighting, 24–28 February, coalition forces ejected the Iraqi army from Kuwait and occupied a large portion of southern Iraq.[31]

The cost to Iraq in terms of personnel and materiel, not to mention national pride, was high. According to U.S. estimates, revised and updated two years after the war, the Iraqis lost 76 percent of their tanks in theater

---

28. Richard W. Stewart, *War in the Persian Gulf: Operations Desert Shield and Desert Storm, August 1990–March 1991* (Washington, DC: U.S. Army Center of Military History, 2010), 69. For the growth of the Third Army/ARCENT staff, see Robert H. Scales Jr., *Certain Victory: The United States Army in the Gulf War* (Washington, DC: Office of the Chief of Staff, United States Army, 1993), 60; Swain, *"Lucky War,"* 43–44.
29. Yeosock, "H+100," 47.
30. Kevin M. Woods, *The Mother of All Battles: Saddam Hussein's Strategic Plan for the Persian Gulf War* (Annapolis, MD: Naval Institute Press, 2008), xv.
31. J. Travis Moger, "The Gulf War at 30," *Army History* 118 (Winter 2021): 6–25.

M1A1 Abrams tanks and M998 Humvees of the 3d Brigade, 1st Armored Division, of the VII Corps, move across the desert in northern Kuwait during Operation DESERT STORM.
(National Archives)

as well as 55 percent of their armored personnel carriers and 90 percent of their artillery. Only five to seven Iraqi combat divisions remained capable of offensive operations.[32] Some units escaped largely intact, such as the *Republican Guard*'s *Hammurabi Division*, while others were so badly damaged that the Iraqi army disbanded them after the war. Iraqi personnel losses were high as well. The coalition killed between 25,000 and 50,000 Iraqi soldiers and captured another 80,000.[33] In contrast, 245 coalition troops were killed in action, including 143 Americans. These casualty numbers included ninety-three U.S. Army soldiers, twenty-eight of whom perished in a single Scud missile attack on a camp in Dhahran, Saudi Arabia.[34] Considering the size and scope of the operation, these figures were remarkably low. They fell far below American prewar casualty estimates in the thousands and seemed to validate a new method of technologically advanced warfare.[35]

---

32. For equipment lost, see Anthony H. Cordesman, "Iraq's Military Forces: 1988–1993," Center for Strategic and International Studies, 1 Sep 1994, 82, https://www.csis.org/analysis/iraqs-military-forces-1988-1993. For division capability, see Schubert and Kraus, *Whirlwind War*, 201.

33. Stephen A. Bourque, *Jayhawk!: The VII Corps in the Persian Gulf War* (Washington, DC: U.S. Army Center of Military History, 2002), 455. Numbers of enemy prisoners vary widely. One U.S. Army Center of Military History publication estimates the total at 60,000. Schubert and Kraus, *Whirlwind War*, 201.

34. For U.S. military casualty information, see "U.S. Military Casualties – Persian Gulf War Casualty Summary Desert Storm (as of 15 February 2021)," Defense Casualty Analysis System, 15 Feb 2021, https://dcas.dmdc.osd.mil/dcas/pages/report_gulf_storm.xhtml. For coalition casualties, see Joel D. Rayburn and Frank K. Sobchak, eds., *The U.S. Army in the Iraq War: Invasion, Insurgency, Civil War, 2003–2006*, vol. 1 (Carlisle, PA: U.S. Army War College Press, 2019), 1. For more on the Scud attack, see Swain, *"Lucky War,"* 241.

35. According to one source, "many predicted military catastrophe or thousands of

The Third Army's responsibilities did not end with the cease-fire. In the wake of combat operations, this headquarters assumed responsibility for three very different missions: (1) occupy southeastern Iraq until Baghdad complied with agreed terms and a UN cease-fire and observer force was in place; (2) provide emergency support to Kuwait until relieved by the Department of Defense Reconstruction Assistance Office, which happened at the end of April; and (3) begin redeploying forces immediately.[36] To make Kuwait safe again, the Third Army destroyed hundreds of pieces of equipment that the fleeing Iraqi units had abandoned. Ordnance removal continued for years. The Third Army helped the UN Iraq-Kuwait Observer Mission establish a 15-kilometer demilitarized zone along the Iraq-Kuwait border.[37] It also provided food, water, shelter, and medical care to displaced Iraqis and assisted with the relocation of 20,000 Iraqi civilians to a refugee camp in Saudi Arabia.[38]

Unlike the clear battlefield results of the Gulf War, the strategic outcomes were mixed. For the U.S. Army, the victory over Iraq proved the basic soundness of its AirLand Battle doctrine, developed after the Vietnam War for conventional warfare and oriented on the European theater.[39] It also justified the Army's investment in new military hardware in the 1970s and 1980s, including what were known as the Big Five: the Abrams tank, the Apache attack helicopter, the Bradley fighting vehicle, the Patriot missile system, and the Black Hawk utility helicopter. The war validated the Army's comprehensive training in maneuver warfare. Realistic, force-on-force exercises at the National Training Center in the Mojave Desert of California honed tactical skills at the brigade level and below, while the computer-simulated war games of the Battle Command Training Program afforded general officers and their staffs opportunities

---

casualties." Department of Defense (DoD), *Conduct of the Persian Gulf War*, Final Rpt to Cong., 10 Apr 1992 (Washington, DC: Government Publishing Office, 1992), ix. Another source reported that "American casualty forecasts as high as 30,000 were made in public." Swain *"Lucky War,"* xxvi. General H. Norman Schwarzkopf Jr. recalled that "the SAMS [School of Advanced Military Studies] team had predicted (rather optimistically, I thought) eight thousand wounded and two thousand dead for the U.S. forces, and that didn't include possible mass casualties from chemical weapons, which were impossible to estimate." H. Norman Schwarzkopf Jr. with Peter Petre, *It Doesn't Take a Hero: The Autobiography* (New York: Bantam, 1992), 356.

36. Swain, *"Lucky War,"* 9.

37. Background information provided by the United Nations (UN) states that "the DMZ, which is about 200 kilometres (125 miles) long, extends 10 kilometres (6 miles) into Iraq and 5 kilometres (3 miles) into Kuwait. Except for the oilfields and two towns—Umm Qasr, which became Iraq's only outlet to the sea, and Safwan—the zone is barren and almost uninhabited." "Iraq/Kuwait – UNIKOM – Background," UN Iraq-Kuwait Observation Mission, UN, https://peacekeeping.un.org/mission/past/unikom/background.html.

38. Yeosock, "H+100," 58.

39. Bourque, *Jayhawk!*, 460; Scales, *Certain Victory*, 25–27. Swain writes, "The ground offensive was planned and conducted in accordance with the Army's AirLand Battle doctrine." Swain, *"Lucky War,"* 72. For the original AirLand Battle doctrine, see U.S. Department of the Army, Field Manual 100–5, *Operations* (Washington, DC: U.S. Department of the Army, 1982).

to test their abilities against experienced opposition force controllers.[40] DESERT STORM also established the usefulness of the post-Vietnam Total Force policy, which drove the military services to integrate their active and reserve components.[41] One in four U.S. military members who deployed to Southwest Asia in support of the Gulf War came from the reserve component and contributed to its successful outcome.[42] The proportion of reservists was even greater for ARCENT, where "more than half of its personnel and units were assigned to the reserve component."[43]

However, some results of the war proved less satisfying. By 1990, 42 percent of the Army's combat divisions were in the National Guard, but the lead time needed to prepare these units for actual combat meant that few of them made it into the fight. Many support units served in the war, but the only major Army National Guard combat units to see action were two field artillery brigades.[44] Had the war or its aftermath lasted longer, reserve combat units might have played a greater role. The actual outcome, however, cast doubt on the wisdom of relying on reserve forces for combat duty. During the Cold War, reserve combat units were used as a strategic reserve, which relied on long lead times for successful activation. The post–Cold War downsizing of active forces, however, led to an earlier reliance on reserves in subsequent conflicts—a demand that was hard to meet.

Ground force operational command and control, which the CENTCOM commander reserved for himself, proved problematic. Although Army doctrine allowed a joint forces commander to appoint a subordinate land forces commander, General Schwarzkopf's decision not to delegate this role was neither unprecedented nor unwarranted. Generals Dwight D. Eisenhower and William C. Westmoreland had served as their own ground component commanders in Europe and Vietnam, respectively.[45] Schwarzkopf's main reason for retaining the joint ground command was roughly the same as Westmoreland's: to avoid offending the host nation by putting its ground forces under a subordinate U.S.

---

40. Scales, *Certain Victory*, 20–23.

41. Brig. Gen. Robert H. Scales Jr., director of the Desert Storm Study Project, notes that "by the late eighties, the Total Force Policy had been so firmly embedded in the Army's structure that 52 percent of combat forces and 67 percent of other forces were Guard or Reserve." Scales, *Certain Victory*, 18.

42. Forrest L. Marion and Jon T. Hoffman, *Forging a Total Force: The Evolution of the Guard and Reserve* (Washington, DC: Historical Office, Office of the Secretary of Defense, 2018), 69.

43. Yeosock, "H+100," 46.

44. Marion and Hoffman, *Forging a Total Force*, 75.

45. To summarize, "General Eisenhower retained overall ground command as well as supreme command, but he delegated control through General Montgomery until September 1944." And also, "General William Westmoreland served from 1964 to 1968 as both commander of the sub-unified U.S. Military Assistance Command Vietnam under U.S. Pacific Command and commander of U.S. Army Vietnam (USARV)." John A. Bonin, "Unified and Joint Land Operations: Doctrine for Landpower," *Land Warfare Papers*, no. 102 (Aug 2014): 2, 4.

command.[46] However, without an overall land component commander below the CINCCENT, coordination among the U.S. Army, Marine Corps, and Arab divisions did not function as smoothly as it could have in the Gulf War. This disjointed command-and-control structure, inherent to coalition warfare, may have contributed to the failure to destroy the *Republican Guard*.[47]

Although the coalition had badly mauled Saddam's forces, President Bush's decision to call a cease-fire after a hundred hours of ground combat allowed the Iraqi army to survive and remain a threat in the region. Even though it had been no match for the international coalition of 700,000 troops, the Iraqi army was powerful enough after the cease-fire—even with the Iraqi economy in shambles and an arms embargo in place—to protect the regime and quell widespread domestic unrest. The Iraqi military could do little to rebuild or modernize after the Gulf War, but it still threatened Iraq's neighbors, especially Kuwait, once most coalition forces departed the region.[48]

---

46. Bonin, "Unified and Joint Land Operations," 6; Swain, *"Lucky War,"* 330. Bonin also mentioned Schwarzkopf's desire to avoid offending the U.S. Marine Corps by placing marine forces under an Army land forces commander. "In addition, the Marines opposed the concept of a JFLCC [joint force land component commander] as they did not want to be dismembered by the two functional components: joint force air component commander (JFACC) and JFLCC." Bonin, "Unified and Joint Land Operations," 7.

47. Mark H. Stroman, "The Gulf War: Operational Leadership and the Failure to Destroy the Republican Guard," (Thesis, Naval War College, 2001), 4, https://apps.dtic.mil/dtic/tr/fulltext/u2/a395087.pdf; Bonin, "Unified and Joint Land Operations," 6; Bourque, *Jayhawk!*, 458; Swain, *"Lucky War,"* 330.

48. The 3 April 1991 UN Security Council omnibus cease-fire resolution left the arms embargo in place. UN Security Council, Resolution 687, Iraq-Kuwait, S/RES/687, 3 Apr 1991, http://unscr.com/en/resolutions/doc/687. Compare to S/RES/661.

UPRISINGS AND REPRESSION IN IRAQ AFTER THE GULF WAR

In the month following the Gulf War cease-fire, popular uprisings in Iraq's Shi'a south and Kurdish north challenged Saddam's regime. Retreating Iraqi soldiers reportedly began an *intifada* (uprising) in the southern Iraqi city of Al Basrah on 1 March when "a soldier, in a fit of anger, turned the gun of his tank in Sa'd Square on an outsized portrait of Saddam."[49] At the peak of the unrest, rebellion engulfed fourteen of Iraq's eighteen provinces. Only the central provinces around Baghdad were unaffected. The Shi'a rebels in southern Iraq received no international support other than limited help from Iran. Using ground combat units and helicopter gunships, the Iraqi government cracked down on the insurgents. Pleas from Shi'a in the south to nearby coalition forces went unheeded. As Saddam's forces quelled the uprising with lethal force, refugees flowed into coalition areas for protection, medical care, water, food, and shelter. In the south, the regime had largely suppressed the rebellion by the end of March.

While the Iraqi army was preoccupied with the uprising in the south, the Kurds in the north used the vulnerability of the postwar Baathist

A U.S. Army UH–60 Black Hawk helicopter flies over northern Iraq in support of Operation PROVIDE COMFORT.

(National Archives)

---

49. Marr, *Modern History of Iraq*, 228. See also Woods, *Mother of All Battles*, 9.

government to push for independence. The Peshmerga seized key cities, including Kirkuk and its large oil fields. The Iraqi military response, which began on 28 March 1991, was swift, bloody, and indiscriminate. Recent memories of attempted Iraqi genocide against the Kurds in 1988, the last year of the Iran-Iraq War, caused close to a million Kurds and other refugees to flee across the mountains to the borders with Turkey and Iran, creating a massive refugee crisis. Eventually, two million Kurds became refugees, roughly half the Kurdish population of Iraq.

Although the international community turned its back on the Shi'a in the south because of concerns about their potential affiliation with revolutionary Iran, it mobilized to help the Kurds in the north. On 5 April, the UN Security Council condemned Iraq for the repression of its civilian population.[50] The following day the United States, in coordination with Great Britain and France, launched Operation Provide Comfort to give protection, shelter, food, water, and medical care to Kurdish

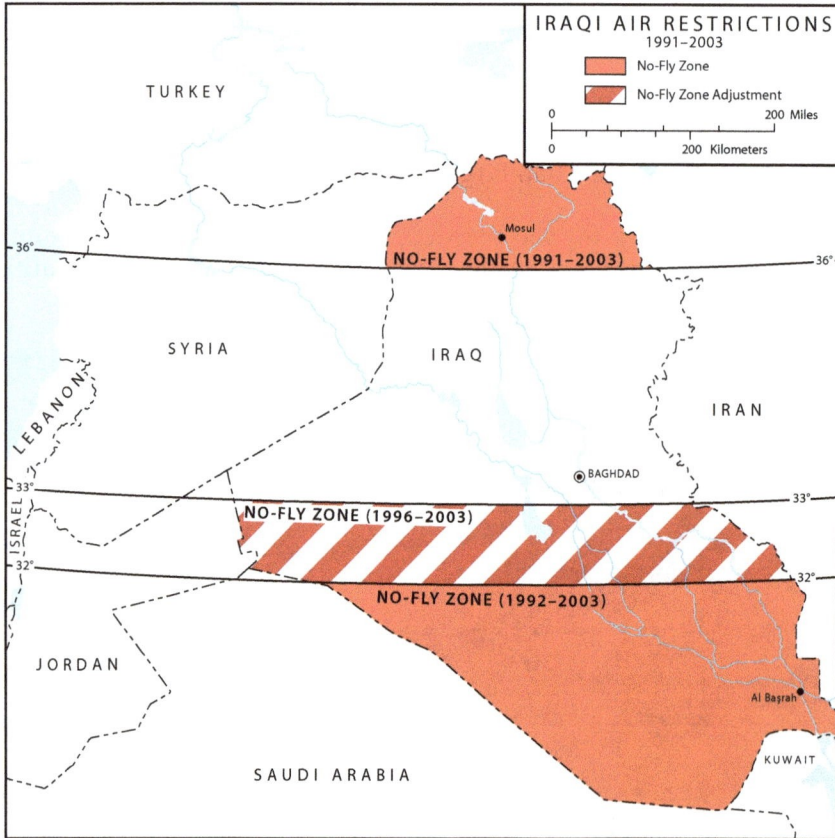

IRAQI AIR RESTRICTIONS
1991–2003

No-Fly Zone

No-Fly Zone Adjustment

Map 5

---

50. For the text of the resolution, see UN Security Council, Resolution 688, Iraq, S/RES/688, 5 Apr 1991, http://unscr.com/en/resolutions/doc/688.

refugees, thus mitigating the crisis. To run the humanitarian operations, U.S. European Command established Joint Task Force (JTF) PROVIDE COMFORT at Incirlik Air Base in Adana, Turkey.[51] Though not explicitly authorized to do so by UN resolution, the United States created a no-fly zone north of the 36th parallel to protect the Kurds from Iraqi air strikes (*Map 5*).[52]

Lt. Gen. John M. D. Shalikashvili, Deputy Commander in Chief, U.S. European Command, assumed command of the JTF on 18 April when the focus shifted from humanitarian *assistance*, mainly air drops of food and water, to humanitarian *intervention* involving coalition ground forces.[53] On 19 April, the general met with Iraqi military representatives and told them coalition forces would create a security zone in the north. He ordered the Iraqi military to withdraw 30 kilometers to the south, beyond artillery range.

General Shalikashvili

Facing a threat of renewed violence, the Iraqi military ceded control of the northern part of the country, and refugees began returning home. Under the protection of ground and air forces provided by a U.S.-led coalition, Kurdish Peshmerga seized and held several towns in northern Iraq. By October, the Iraqi government reached a cease-fire agreement with the Kurds, and the Iraqi military permanently withdrew behind a defensible line. Saddam abandoned his country's northern territories—with the exception of Kirkuk and its oil field—to Kurdish control. The government's acceptance of this stalemate ended the northern intifada, but the U.S.-led coalition continued to enforce the no-fly zone as a way to help the Kurds maintain their autonomy.

---

51. Perry D. Jamieson, "Northern Iraq," Airmen at War Articles, Air Force Historical Research Agency, 30 Sep 2015, 2, https://www.afhra.af.mil/Airmen-At-War/. Because of the participation of the British and French militaries, the Joint Task Force (JTF) PROVIDE COMFORT commander, Air Forces Maj. Gen. James L. Jamerson, quickly redesignated the headquarters *Combined* Task Force (CTF) PROVIDE COMFORT. Ibid., 3.
52. President George H. W. Bush announced, "The prohibition against Iraqi fixed- and rotary-wing aircraft flying north of the 36th parallel remains in effect." Press Bfg, President George H. W. Bush, "Iraqi Refugee Situation," 16 Apr 1991, https://www.c-span.org/video/?17573-1/iraqi-refugee-situation.
53. Scales, *Certain Victory*, 341; Gordon W. Rudd, *Humanitarian Intervention: Assisting the Iraqi Kurds in Operation PROVIDE COMFORT, 1991* (Washington, DC: U.S. Army Center of Military History, 2004), 107.

After the Gulf War, the Army focused on budget cuts and the resulting personnel drawdowns in line with Congress's pursuit of a post–Cold War "peace dividend."[54] The demobilization of the Cold War army in Europe, which had begun in 1990, accelerated after the Gulf War ended the following year. Over the next decade, Army Chiefs of Staff General Gordon R. Sullivan, General Dennis J. Reimer, and General Eric K. Shinseki oversaw a dramatic drawdown of forces. Some units that fought in the desert returned to Germany only to be inactivated shortly thereafter, including the 3d Armored Division and the VII Corps. The number of active duty divisions fell from eighteen to ten. Not for the first time, the Army made disproportional cuts in its force structure in order to maintain its combat power. As a result of the 1996 Quadrennial Defense Review, the Army cut support troops—15,000 from the active component and 45,000 from the reserves—creating an imbalanced force with a degraded ability to sustain ground combat forces.[55] The Army's active duty personnel strength dropped throughout the 1990s. From an authorized strength of approximately 771,000 in 1989 (already 8,800 fewer than the previous year), the Army's total force dipped below 481,000 soldiers in 2001, the lowest it had been since 1940.[56] Similarly, the Army's budget declined throughout the 1990s, from $78.9 billion in 1989 to a low of $60.4 billion in 1998.[57]

In light of congressionally mandated fiscal constraints and new post–Cold War realities, the Army of the 1990s became primarily, but not exclusively, an expeditionary force based in the continental United States.

---

54. John S. Brown, *Kevlar Legions: The Transformation of the U.S. Army, 1989–2005* (Washington, DC: U.S. Army Center of Military History, 2011), 73–74, 75, 172, 301, 349, 481.
55. Brown, *Kevlar Legions*, 166; Stephen D. Kidder, "War Planning with Missing Pieces: How We Made It Work" (Unpublished paper, Carlisle, PA: Center for Strategic Leadership, U.S. Army War College, n.d.), 22, Historians Files, CMH. Similar situations developed after previous U.S. wars as Army leaders preserved combat strength at the expense of combat support and combat service support units.
56. Vincent H. Demma, *Department of the Army Historical Summary (DAHSUM), Fiscal Year (FY) 1989* (Washington, DC: U.S. Army Center of Military History, 1998), 109; Christopher N. Koontz, *DAHSUM, FY 2001* (Washington, DC: U.S. Army Center of Military History, 2011), 12. Compare to DoD, *Selected Manpower Statistics, Fiscal Year 1997* (Washington, DC: U.S. Government Printing Office, 1997), 50, table 2.11.
57. Demma, *DAHSUM, FY 1989*, 40; W. Blair Haworth Jr., *DAHSUM, FY 1998* (Washington, DC: U.S. Army Center of Military History, 2005), 19; W. Blair Haworth Jr., *DAHSUM, FY 2000* (Washington, DC: U.S. Army Center of Military History, 2011), 12.

Overseas presence decreased dramatically, with only 118,000 soldiers stationed abroad in 1994, compared to almost 250,000 from five years earlier.[58] This new U.S.-based approach required improved infrastructure at military installations, increased strategic airlift and sealift, and robust pre-positioning of materiel both on land and aboard ships. The Army expanded and modernized loading and cargo handling facilities at key U.S. bases that it designated as "power projection platforms," strategically located near major seaports and airports.[59]

Learning from its Gulf War experience, the Army augmented pre-positioned stockpiles to support the rapid deployment of heavy forces. Stockpiling materiel was not a new concept. The Army had maintained pre-positioned war reserves in Western Europe since the early 1960s.[60] In 1993, the Department of the Army turned over the management of the Army War Reserve (AWR) program to U.S. Army Materiel Command (AMC).[61] To support contingency operations in the CENTCOM area of operations, AMC managed two stockpiles. One, known as AWR-3, was afloat at the island of Diego Garcia in the Indian Ocean. The other, known as AWR-5, was ashore at Camp Doha, Kuwait.[62] In March 1995, AWR-5 expanded to include a second site in Qatar. Each of these stockpiles—in Kuwait, Qatar, and Diego Garcia—eventually contained equipment for a heavy brigade, achieving CENTCOM's goal to pre-position a full heavy division's worth of equipment in the region. Airlift, sealift, and pre-positioned equipment formed the triad of strategic mobility that enabled the deterrence operations of the 1990s.

58. Gordon R. Sullivan, *The Collected Works of the Thirty-Second Chief of Staff, United States Army, June 1991–June 1994* (Washington, DC: Department of the Army, n.d.), 434.
59. Historical Ofc, U.S. Army Materiel Cmd, *Operation Iraqi Freedom: "It Was A Pre-positioned War"* (Fort Belvoir, VA: U.S. Army Materiel Command, [2004]), 5.
60. Donald A. Carter, *Forging the Shield: The U.S. Army in Europe, 1951–1962*, U.S. Army in the Cold War (Washington, DC: U.S. Army Center of Military History, 2011), 427–28.
61. In June 1997, Army leadership changed the name to Army Pre-positioned Stocks. Annual Cmd History, FY 1997, U.S. Army Materiel Cmd, n.d., Annual History Rpt Collection, CMH; Memo, Lt. Gen. John G. Boburn, Deputy Chief of Staff for Logistics, for Commander, U.S. Army Materiel Command, and Commander, U.S. Army Medical Materiel Agency, 18 Jun 1997, subject (sub): Name Change for Army War Reserves, 1, Historians Files, CMH. Headquarters, Department of the Army, retained ownership of the Army War Reserve program.
62. A territory of the United Kingdom, Diego Garcia is an atoll in the Indian Ocean halfway between East Africa and Southeast Asia. The British government expelled the local inhabitants in the late 1960s and early 1970s and leased the island to the United States, which built Navy and Air Force bases there. The 2-mile-long runway can accommodate long-range bombers and the 80-square-mile, deep-water lagoon can berth more than two dozen warships. Shashank Bengali, "A Half-Century After Being Uprooted for a Remote U.S. Naval Base, These Islanders Are Still Fighting to Return," *Los Angeles Times*, 14 Aug 2018, https://www.latimes.com/world/africa/la-fg-britain-us-diego-garcia-20180814-story.html.

UNITED NATIONS SANCTIONS AND WEAPONS INSPECTIONS

After the end of the Gulf War, the UN Security Council set the conditions for ending economic sanctions, including an oil embargo, imposed after Iraq invaded Kuwait in 1990.[63] Iraq would have to recognize its pre-invasion border with Kuwait and dismantle its WMD programs under international supervision. The Security Council established a new weapons inspections regime, the UN Special Commission (UNSCOM), to verify Iraq's compliance with the resolution. UNSCOM was responsible for overseeing the identification and destruction of Iraq's biological and chemical weapons, as well as its long-range missiles. The UN assigned the dismantlement of Iraq's suspected nuclear weapons program to the International Atomic Energy Agency (IAEA).[64]

From the beginning, Iraq played a cat-and-mouse game with UN weapons inspectors, putting obstacles in their path, obfuscating information, and pushing the limits of tolerable behavior. In June 1991, Iraqi personnel fired warning shots in the air to scare off inspectors.[65] Three months later, Iraqi officials prevented an inspection team from leaving a site with documents related to Iraq's nuclear weapons program. After a four-day stand-off, Iraqi officials allowed the inspectors to leave with the documents only after the UN Security Council threatened enforcement by its member states.

Despite Iraq's partial and grudging compliance, the IAEA weapons inspectors made progress. Between 1991 and 1994, they identified and dismantled about forty nuclear research facilities and three secret uranium-enrichment programs. UNSCOM destroyed more than 148,000 tons of chemical weapons, including both blister agents (such as sulfur mustard) and nerve agents (such as sarin and tabun).[66] This substantial but incomplete progress formed the basis for an Iraqi push to end economic sanctions.

63. S/RES/687. Compare to Daniel Byman, "After the Storm: U.S. Policy Toward Iraq Since 1991," *Political Science Quarterly* 115, no. 4 (Winter 2000–2001): 504.
64. Hans Blix, *Disarming Iraq* (New York: Pantheon, 2004), 20.
65. Anthony H. Cordesman, *Iraq and the War of Sanctions: Conventional Threats and Weapons of Mass Destruction* (Westport, CT: Praeger, 1999), 184.
66. Marr, *Modern History of Iraq*, 237.

THE U.S. ARMY AND THE RECONSTRUCTION OF KUWAIT

Planning for a postconflict Kuwait began soon after Iraq invaded the emirate in August 1990. Policymakers and defense officials in Washington realized the importance of rebuilding the country as quickly as possible after expelling the Iraqi army. Otherwise, they risked winning the war but losing the peace. The process was complicated, because planners could not predict whether Saddam would withdraw his forces or fight for Kuwait. U.S. Army civil affairs experts worked with their Kuwaiti counterparts in the newly created Kuwait Emergency Response Program to prepare for the worst. They stockpiled supplies in Saudi Arabia and contracted for services to meet anticipated needs. Until the Iraqi army evacuated Kuwait and conditions were safe enough for Kuwaiti expatriates to return, the U.S. Army would execute all emergency response operations. Because they provided the funding, the Kuwaitis would continue to approve all contracts.

When war with Iraq appeared certain in January 1991, CENTCOM designated the Third Army/ARCENT to oversee all DESERT STORM civil-military missions, directing the headquarters "to provide all necessary emergency food, water, medical care and supplies, temporary shelter, and public services after the liberation of Kuwait."[67] To carry out these missions, ARCENT created the Combined Civil Affairs Task Force. The task force consisted of soldiers from the 352d Civil Affairs Command and personnel from other services, foreign militaries, and nongovernmental organizations. Because the Combined Civil Affairs Task Force lacked critical engineering, project management, and contracting capabilities, ARCENT combined the task force with the Kuwait Emergency Recovery Office, a U.S. Army Corps of Engineers entity, on 20 February. The resulting new umbrella organization, Task Force FREEDOM, reported to ARCENT (Forward) and operated out of the Third Army mobile command post.

As the Iraqi army retreated from Kuwait during the last week of February 1991, it abandoned military equipment, left minefields on land and sea, set oil wells on fire, and looted hospitals and other facilities. Without electricity, the country remained in darkness, and raw sewage flowed into the Persian Gulf. Dark clouds of smoke billowed from oil fires, limiting visibility and coating everything in oily soot. U.S. soldiers

---

67. Janet A. McDonnell, *After DESERT STORM: The U.S. Army and the Reconstruction of Kuwait* (Washington, DC: Department of the Army, 1999), 49.

43

reported having to drive with headlights on in the middle of the day. Coalition bombing had caused extensive damage, and craters pockmarked roads, making some impassible. Bombed-out buildings marred Kuwait City's once-gleaming skyline. Deadly unexploded ordnance littered the countryside.

To assure Kuwaitis of the United States' ongoing commitment to the defense of their country, CENTCOM ordered the 1st Brigade, 3d Armored Division, to remain behind temporarily as a security force.[68] This brigade, organized as a tank-infantry force, formed the core of the task-organized 3d Armored Division (Forward), which included various other units from the division.[69] Utilizing American equipment left behind after the war, this brigade relocated to Kuwait City on 12 May 1991 "to occupy assembly areas as the theater reserve, provide a continued U.S. presence in Kuwait to deter further aggression, and prepare to counterattack and destroy any Iraqi penetration of the demilitarized zone."[70] Like Task Force FREEDOM, the 3d Armored Division (Forward) fell under ARCENT (Forward) for its new deterrence mission, Operation POSITIVE FORCE. In June 1991, elements of the 11th Armored Cavalry deployed from Germany to Kuwait where they relieved the 3d Armored Division and became Task Force VICTORY.[71] The 11th ACR remained until September 1991 when the 3d Battalion, 77th Armor, took over the mission and equipment, occupying Camp Doha and, farther north, Camp Monterey. The latter facility was located only 11 kilometers from the Iraqi border, within sight of the oil well fires that were still burning six months after the war.[72]

Task Force VICTORY II—assembled around 3d Battalion, 77th Armor, during its POSITIVE FORCE mission—conducted the first U.S.-Kuwaiti training exercise after the Gulf War in which Kuwaiti armored companies went through "a scenario that included a passage of [one unit through another's] lines and a thirty-kilometer counterattack across a training area still littered with destroyed vehicles from the DESERT STORM fighting."[73] The reduced threat from Iraq after the war's end allowed the United States to

---

68. Secretary of Defense Richard B. Cheney "emphasized that the United States had no intention of permanently stationing ground forces in the Persian Gulf and that the deployment from Europe simply met a temporary need to provide security while the government of Kuwait reconstituted its own forces." Charles E. Kirkpatrick, "Ruck It Up!": The Post–Cold War Transformation of V Corps, 1990–2001 (Washington, DC: Department of the Army, 2006), 174.
69. Kirkpatrick, "Ruck It Up!," 172.
70. Kirkpatrick, "Ruck It Up!," 172.
71. As an armored cavalry regiment, 11th Armored Cavalry was commonly referred to as 11th ACR.
72. The 3d Battalion, 77th Armor (Task Force 3–77), arrived in Kuwait at the end of August 1991. At the end of November, the unit returned to Germany. Kirkpatrick, "Ruck It Up!," 182.
73. Kirkpatrick, "Ruck It Up!," 182.

cancel Operation POSITIVE FORCE at the end of 1991 in favor of a recurring exercise program that would begin almost a year later.[74]

While Army maneuver units engaged in deterrence operations and trained the Kuwaiti military, the members of Task Force FREEDOM executed their mission to provide emergency support for the first ninety days after the end of hostilities. Damage assessment teams conducted thousands of site visits, assessing damages and evaluating humanitarian needs. The task force had to work with limited resources to support the Kuwaiti people and repair the country's destroyed infrastructure. Civil affairs personnel distributed water, food, and medicine, and housed the many displaced persons who had lost their homes and livelihoods in the war. Engineers labored to remove debris and unexploded ordnance; restore electricity, water, sewer, and telecommunications networks; and open roads, ports, and airports. Despite the difficult conditions and the enormous amount of work to be done, Task Force FREEDOM established an impressive record of accomplishments by the time it completed its mission, a month ahead of schedule, on 30 April 1991. Working with their Kuwaiti counterparts, the task force restored power to the entire country in less than a month, and provided 12,500 metric tons of food, 12.8 million liters of water, 1,250 tons of medical supplies, and two truckloads of medical equipment.[75]

At the end of April 1991, the effort in Kuwait shifted from the response to the recovery phase, and Task Force FREEDOM turned over its responsibilities to the Defense Reconstruction Assistance Office.[76] The Kuwait Emergency Recovery Office reported to this new organization. Over the next eight months, the two organizations finished repairing Kuwait's damaged infrastructure.

The reconstruction work took place through contracts, which allowed the United States to draw on corporate expertise from around the world and kept the number of uniformed U.S. military personnel in Kuwait low, avoiding the appearance of a military occupation. This approach built good will with Kuwaitis, who allowed the U.S. military to keep a small force, mostly civilian, at Camp Doha and to pre-position some military equipment there.[77] It also provided a boon to American businesses. U.S. politicians convinced the Kuwaitis to award contracts in proportion to the number of troops each coalition nation contributed. This system guaranteed that American firms would secure the most contracts. To run Camp Doha, the Army established U.S. Army Training and Security, Kuwait, in October 1991. This command became U.S. Army Central Command, Kuwait, in November 1995.[78]

---

74. Kirkpatrick, *"Ruck It Up!,"* 184.
75. McDonnell, *After DESERT STORM,* 97.
76. Yeosock, "H+100," 58.
77. The arrangement with Kuwait was meant to be temporary, but the United States has maintained a presence in Kuwait ever since.
78. Historical Data Card, Unit W47TAA, Force Structure and Unit History, Field

One of the biggest tasks entrusted to American contractors was fighting oil fires. The Iraqi army had devastated Kuwait's oil infrastructure as soldiers withdrew to Iraq. In her book, *After DESERT STORM: The U.S. Army and the Reconstruction of Kuwait*, Janet A. McDonnell explained, "They blew up over 600 oil wells, resulting in the loss of 5 to 6 million barrels per day. Roughly 520, or 85 percent, of the wells burned at temperatures as high as 2,000 degrees Fahrenheit. The rest gushed thousands of barrels of crude oil into large, dark, lifeless 'lakes,' up to six feet deep."[79] The Kuwait government contracted with three U.S. companies—Red Adair, Boots and Coots, and Wild Well Control—plus one Canadian firm, Safety Boss, to fight the oil fires. They also hired construction giant Bechtel to rebuild oil infrastructure and provide housing, food, and other support to firefighters.

Work began slowly because it took time to get the necessary equipment and life support in place. Initial estimates suggested it could take two years to cap all the blown wells. On 7 April 1991, Boots and Coots extinguished the first oil well fire. Seven months later, in November, firefighters put out the final blaze. Through the efforts of the U.S. Army, contractors, and the Kuwaitis themselves, the biggest environmental and economic disaster of the war was finally over. On 1 December 1991, the Defense Reconstruction Assistance Office closed, and Secretary of Defense Richard B. "Dick" Cheney ended the Army's executive agency for the reconstruction of Kuwait. The rebuilding efforts concluded more quickly and efficiently than predicted. However, subsequent events would demonstrate that, despite these tidy details, the Gulf War had anything but a clean ending.

Programs Directorate, CMH.
79. McDonnell, *After DESERT STORM*, 183.

Iraq's military continued to harass many Iraqi civilians long after it had suppressed the 1991 intifada. The regime in Baghdad viewed both the Kurds and the Shi'a as ongoing threats. Reports of Iraqi aircraft bombing and strafing Shi'a villages prompted the United States, with the support of Great Britain and France, to establish a no-fly zone in the south of Iraq similar to the one protecting Kurds in the north. (*See Map 5, page 36.*) The stated purpose of this action was to enforce the UN resolution that demanded an immediate end to repression of the Iraqi people.[80] President Bush announced Operation SOUTHERN WATCH on 26 August 1992 to enforce the new no-fly zone south of latitude 32° north. The exclusion area—called "The Box" by SOUTHERN WATCH participants—was roughly the size of Iowa. CENTCOM created Joint Task Force SOUTHWEST ASIA (JTF SWA) in Riyadh, Saudi Arabia, to run the operation, and Headquarters, Ninth U.S. Air Force, based at Shaw Air Force Base in South Carolina, executed the mission. The Ninth Air Force, CENTCOM's Air Force component, had a forward headquarters in Riyadh.[81] Coalition fighters and other aircraft of the 4404th Composite Wing flew patrol missions seven days a week from Dhahran Air Base in Saudi Arabia.

In October 1992, as the Air Force was patrolling the exclusion zone over southern Iraq, the Army began a recurring Kuwaiti-American training exercise called INTRINSIC ACTION. To control Army forces participating in these exercises, the Third Army had temporarily established Joint Task Force–Kuwait (JTF-Kuwait) three months earlier.[82] This task force would be activated and inactivated as needed. Three times a year, an Army heavy task force—often from either the 1st Cavalry or 24th Infantry Division (later reflagged as the 3d Infantry Division)—deployed to Kuwait as a show of force and a warning to

---

80. S/RES/688.

81. Many contemporary documents refer to the Ninth Air Force as Central Air Forces or CENTAF. This was never part of the headquarters' name. The Air Force added the designation Air Forces Central or AFCENT to the unit name HQ [Headquarters] Ninth Air Force on 1 March 2008. SO GB–45, Department of the Air Force, HQ, Air Combat Cmd, 29 Feb 2008, Historians Files, CMH. The official designation changed again on 5 August 2009 to "HQ [Headquarters] United States Air Forces Central Command—(USAFCENT)." SO GB–99, Department of the Air Force, HQ, Air Combat Cmd, 4 Aug 2009, Historians Files, CMH.

82. Stephen E. Everett and L. Martin Kaplan, *DAHSUM, FY 1993* (Washington, DC: U.S. Army Center of Military History, 2002), 55.

Saddam Hussein. An armored or mechanized battalion formed the core of each task force. As in the annual Cold War REFORGER exercises designed to reinforce NATO (North Atlantic Treaty Organization) forces in Europe, Army units practiced a four-fold military operation in Kuwait, including reception, staging, onward movement, and integration. They would draw pre-positioned supplies and equipment at Camp Doha before proceeding in convoys to the Udari Range complex near the Iraqi border to conduct live-fire field training exercises with Kuwaiti units.

With no U.S. combat units permanently stationed in the country, these exercises partially addressed the crucial time-distance problem of deterring Iraq. The U.S. military believed Iraq was capable of launching an attack into Kuwait using three to five divisions from southern Iraq with less than twenty-four hours' warning.[83] Saddam's main advantage was geography. The Iraqi army's supply lines were no more than 500 kilometers long, all overland and with good highways and railroads, whereas the U.S. East Coast was seven time zones away, a distance which turned deterrence operations against Iraq into a recurring race for Kuwait.

Iraq first tested the coalition's resolve not on the ground but in the air. On 27 December 1992, a U.S. F–16 fighter intercepted and shot down an Iraqi MiG–25 Foxbat fighter 20 nautical miles inside the southern no-fly zone after the MiG locked on its radar. In response, Iraq moved surface-to-air missiles into the no-fly zone during the first week of January 1993. Although the deployment of these weapon systems did not violate UN resolutions, it appeared highly provocative. The Bush administration demanded their removal. Iraq refused. Then, on 7 January 1993, the Iraqi government did not allow UN aircraft supporting UNSCOM inspectors to land in Baghdad. The Security Council determined this act to be a material breach of the cease-fire agreement.

Iraqi provocations and coalition responses escalated. On 10 January, Iraq sent about 250 unarmed soldiers, wearing civilian clothes, across the UN-mandated demilitarized zone into Kuwait to retrieve equipment that Iraqi troops had abandoned during the Gulf War, including four Chinese-built Silkworm missiles.[84] Three days later, British and French aircraft struck targets in the southern no-fly zone. Then on 17 January, another U.S. F–16 shot down an Iraqi fighter, this time a MiG–23 Flogger, in the northern exclusion zone. The following night, a U.S. Navy cruise missile attack destroyed an Iraqi nuclear weapons facility at Za'faraniyeh, 20 kilometers south of Baghdad. About this

---

83. End of Tour Rpt, General J. H. Binford Peay III, Cdr in Ch, U.S. Central Command (CENTCOM), 3 Nov 1997, 25; Historians Files, CMH.
84. Perry D. Jamieson, "Southern Iraq," Airmen at War Articles, Air Force Historical Research Agency, 30 Sep 2015, 4, https://www.afhra.af.mil/Airmen-At-War/. See also Gregory Fontenot, *The 1st Infantry Division and the US Army Transformed: Road to Victory in Desert Storm, 1970–1991* (Columbia: University of Missouri Press, 2017), 435.

time, the Army rapidly deployed a task force of approximately 1,100 soldiers from the 1st Cavalry Division in Fort Hood, Texas, to Kuwait and reactivated JTF-Kuwait to control Army forces in the country.[85] A second U.S. raid on missile sites in southern Iraq took place on 18 January, the day after the downing of the MiG–23. Over the next four days—before and after President William J. "Bill" Clinton took office on 20 January—U.S. fighters supporting Operation PROVIDE COMFORT in northern Iraq attacked surface-to-air batteries in northern Iraq that posed a threat to their mission. The timing of Iraq's provocations suggested that Saddam was testing U.S. resolve during the waning days of Bush's tenure in office.

The Clinton administration continued the Bush administration's containment approach toward Iraq and added similar measures against Iran, calling the new regional strategy "dual containment."[86] However, Clinton went beyond containment when he ordered a retaliatory attack on the Iraqi Intelligence Service for trying to assassinate former President Bush during an April 1993 visit to Kuwait. On 26 June 1993, the USS *Peterson*, a Navy destroyer, launched twenty-three Tomahawk cruise missiles from the Red Sea toward downtown Baghdad, hitting the headquarters of the Iraqi Intelligence Service, which the U.S. government believed was behind the assassination attempt. Meanwhile, the U.S. Air Force continued to enforce the exclusion zones over northern and southern Iraq.

Despite an impressive safety record over time, patrolling missions in the two no-fly zones involved significant risk. On 14 April 1995, two U.S. Army UH–60 Black Hawk helicopters and their crews assigned to Operation PROVIDE COMFORT were transporting U.S., British, French, and Turkish military officers, Kurdish representatives, and an American political adviser in northern Iraq.[87] Mistaking the Black Hawks for Russian-made Iraqi aircraft, two American F–15C fighters shot down both helicopters, killing all twenty-six people aboard.

---

85. The task force was built around the 1st Battalion, 9th Cavalry, 1st Cavalry Division. Everett and Kaplan, *DAHSUM, FY 1993*, 56.
86. "These steps are being taken to further all of these objectives and the policy of containing Iraq that I have pursued for 4 years now, and it was developed before me under President Bush." William J. Clinton, *Public Papers of the Presidents of the United States: William J. Clinton, 1996, Book 2* (Washington, DC: Government Printing Office, 1996), 1471. By 1994, the Clinton administration had articulated a policy of "dual containment" toward Iran and Iraq. National Security Advisor W. Anthony K. Lake explained, "In adopting this strategy, we are not oblivious to the need for a balance of power in the region. Rather, we seek with our regional allies to maintain a favorable balance without depending on either Iraq or Iran." Lake, "Confronting Backlash States," 48. Historian David B. Crist observed, "Containing Iran and Iraq would free the Arabs and Israelis to make peace. Then a unified Middle East would help strengthen the containment of Iraq and Iran." Crist, *Twilight War*, 392.
87. Ofc of Special Investigations, U.S. General Accounting Ofc, *Operation Provide Comfort: Review of U.S. Air Force Investigation of Black Hawk Fratricide Incident*, Rpt to Cong., 5 Nov 1997, 2, https://www.gao.gov/assets/160/156037.pdf.

An investigation revealed a series of errors that led to the fratricide, causing military leaders to take corrective actions to prevent similar accidents.[88]

---

88. Ofc of Special Investigations, *Review of U.S. Air Force Investigation*, 5 Nov 1997, 6.

THE U.S. ARMY IN SOMALIA

The Clinton administration's next major foreign policy challenge took place in East Africa. On 26 January 1991, rebel militia groups forced Somali dictator Mohammed Siad Barre to flee the capital, Mogadishu. In the resulting power vacuum, the clan-based nation descended into civil war. To relieve the widespread starvation caused by food shortages and an inadequate food distribution system disrupted by Somali warlords, in April 1992 the UN established United Nations Operations in Somalia (UNOSOM) to provide security for the distribution of relief supplies. However, as the security situation deteriorated, UNOSOM quickly became overwhelmed. At the time, northeast Africa was part of the CENTCOM area of responsibility and under the command of Marine Corps General Joseph P. Hoar. To support UNOSOM relief efforts, CENTCOM began Operation PROVIDE RELIEF in August 1992, the same month it initiated Operation SOUTHERN WATCH. At its height, PROVIDE RELIEF used twenty-four C–130s and more than 1,000 personnel to deliver a total of 26,435 metric tons of supplies.

U.S. involvement in Somalia increased significantly in the following year. Because armed gangs were stealing food intended for starving Somalis, on 4 December 1992 President Bush announced Operation RESTORE HOPE to secure humanitarian food distribution. The Third Army developed the original concept of operations for RESTORE HOPE, which fell under the multinational coalition known as the Unified Task Force (UNITAF), commanded by Marine Corps Lt. Gen. Robert B. Johnson. The U.S. Army component of UNITAF was Task Force MOUNTAIN composed of 10th Mountain Division elements based at Fort Drum, New York. They took responsibility for four sectors in southern Somalia. Just before the end of the year, Maj. Gen. Steven L. Arnold, who had been the Third Army G–3 operations officer during DESERT STORM, took command of the task force. After President Clinton assumed office in January 1993, the U.S. commitment to Somalia continued, changing over time as the situation on the ground evolved. Early 1993 saw an improvement in security and food distribution, allowing the United States to shift from a leading role to a supporting one.

Even while providing plans, troops, and logistical support to units in Somalia, ARCENT met its commitments in the Middle East. For example, it continued to deploy soldiers to the Sinai Peninsula where they served as part of the multinational force and observers (MFO) organization. This international peacekeeping operation grew out of the 1979 Egypt-Israel Peace Treaty, which called for the demilitarization of the Sinai Peninsula.

MFO soldiers operated checkpoints, conducted reconnaissance patrols, and staffed observations posts along the international boundary in the Sinai to observe, report on, and periodically verify the implementation of the treaty. The U.S. element of the MFO, Task Force Sinai, provided approximately 530 personnel on a six-month rotation. Even though the commitment was relatively minimal, the Sinai operation, like all ongoing operations, taxed the Army's readiness in an era of force reductions.[89]

With conditions in Somalia improving and operations costing the United States $100 million per month, the new Clinton administration sought to reduce the U.S. commitment. On 4 May 1993, UNITAF turned over operations to a reconstituted UN authority, UNOSOM II, and Operation RESTORE HOPE became

General Hoar
(U.S. Marine Corps)

Operation CONTINUE HOPE. UNITAF strength had peaked at 38,300 personnel, including 25,800 U.S. forces. In this new phase, only a residual American presence of 4,000 troops remained, including a logistical support command of 2,800 and a quick reaction force of 1,200.[90] Not long after UNOSOM II took over relief operations, security in the Somali capital, Mogadishu, began to deteriorate. One warlord, Somali General Mohammed Farah Aideed, and his Somali National Alliance (SNA) militia were most responsible for the unrest. As Aideed's followers showed increasing hostility to the UNOSOM II forces, U.S. and coalition casualties began to mount. In June, the SNA killed twenty-four Pakistani peacekeepers. On 8 August, four U.S. soldiers were killed when their vehicle struck a command-detonated land mine in Mogadishu. Two weeks later, in response to this attack, President Clinton deployed Task Force RANGER, which included 400 U.S. Army Rangers and Delta Force operators.

Despite the presence of elite American troops, the violence continued. On 25 September, three soldiers from Task Force MOUNTAIN died when Aideed's militiamen shot down their helicopter. This attack emboldened Aideed's supporters to try again. The following month, during a Task Force RANGER raid on one of Aideed's compounds, the SNA shot down two UH–60 Black Hawk helicopters. Dismounted troops and members of a relief convoy came under heavy fire. U.S. casualties numbered eighteen

---

89. Everett and Kaplan, *DAHSUM, FY 1993*, 51–52, 55.
90. Jay E. Hines, *A Brief History of the U.S. Central Command* (MacDill Air Force Base, FL: United States Central Command History Office, Feb 1995), 25–26, Historians Files, CMH.

killed and eighty-one wounded by the time the battle was over.[91] By contrast, U.S. forces inflicted much higher casualties on their adversaries, killing approximately 300 SNA fighters and wounding hundreds more. Two Army special operators, M. Sgt. Gary I. Gordon and Sfc. Randall D. Shughart, received the Medal of Honor posthumously for heroism. The 3–4 October Battle of Mogadishu—immortalized in the book and film *Black Hawk Down*—proved an important turning point in the conflict. In the aftermath of the battle, the U.S. military presence in Somalia surged dramatically, but this increase was temporary.

Although most Americans had supported relief operations early in the mission, the prospect of getting bogged down in a bloody civil war in Africa did not sit well with many, including top lawmakers in Washington. Republican Senator John S. McCain called on the Clinton administration to bring the troops home, citing President Reagan's decision to withdraw from Lebanon in 1984 after militia-backed suicide bombers struck multiple U.S. military and civilian installations in Beirut. Faced with an intractable situation in Somalia and increasing opposition to continuing military operations, President Clinton decided to withdraw all U.S. forces by the

A UH–60 Black Hawk engine from the wreckage of the first helicopter shot down during the Battle of Mogadishu, Somalia

(National Museum of the United States Army)

---

91. Hines, *A Brief History of the U.S. Central Command*, 27. Casualty numbers vary from source to source. The Third Army reported 18 killed in action and 89 wounded in action on the U.S. side. A pamphlet by Richard Stewart mentions 16 killed in action and 57 wounded in action but does not cite a source. Third Army's 18 killed in action include two Army Delta Force operators not in Hines's and Stewart's counts. Annual Historical Review, Third U.S. Army, FY 1993, Exec Sum, 13 Jun 1994, Annual History Rpt Collection, CMH; Richard Stewart, *The United States Army in Somalia, 1992–1994* (Washington, DC: U.S. Army Center of Military History, 2002), 23.

end of March 1994. At the end of 1993, Secretary of Defense Leslie "Les" Aspin Jr. resigned amid widespread criticism for failures in Somalia.

As a result of these experiences in Somalia, many Americans, both military and civilian, soured on the idea of using U.S. troops for peacekeeping duties, at least in Africa. A 1993 Third Army report observed, with regard to operations in Somalia, that "such [humanitarian relief] missions are not the top priority for which Third Army/ARCENT must train and prepare."[92] Not only did peacekeeping lie outside the Army's primary competency, but it also invited a dangerous mission creep. In just a few months' time, what had started as humanitarian relief in Somalia became relief plus security operations, and this in turn expanded to become relief, security, and urban combat.

Despite these concerns, the U.S. military found itself occupied with what were known as military operations other than war throughout the 1990s. Although the United States did not intervene militarily to stop an attempted genocide in the African nations of Rwanda and Burundi in 1994, it did send a modest number of troops to Africa to provide humanitarian assistance after the violence subsided.[93] Though public opinion on using the military for international peacekeeping efforts was not always favorable, President Clinton ordered the Army to deploy peacekeepers in greater numbers to Haiti, Bosnia, and Kosovo. These commitments kept much of Americans' attention diverted from Iraq for most of the time between the Gulf War and the 11 September 2001 attacks, even though the Baathist state remained a threat to its neighbors and continued to resist UN weapons inspectors.

Observing from afar, Saddam Hussein drew his own conclusions from the brief U.S. involvement in Somalia. He confirmed his belief that Americans had a low tolerance for casualties and that inflicting such losses on them could be relatively easy.[94] In Mogadishu, a disorganized militia armed with rocket-propelled grenades and improvised fighting vehicles did enough damage to cause the United States to withdraw its forces. This lesson was not lost on the Iraqis. The tactics used in 1993 by General Aideed's militia inspired those of the Fedayeen Saddam, a paramilitary group which U.S. ground troops would face in Iraq in 2003.

---

92. Annual Historical Review, Third U.S. Army, FY 1993, Exec Sum, 13 Jun 1994.
93. In Operation SUPPORT HOPE, the United States sent 2,400 peacekeepers to Rwanda "to purify water, facilitate humanitarian relief, and secure transportation nodes, but did not play a leading role." Brown, *Kevlar Legions*, 114. See also Kirkpatrick, *"Ruck It Up!,"* 253–71.
94. Kevin M. Woods, *The Iraqi Perspectives Report* (Annapolis, MD: Naval Institute Press, 2006), 29–30. An official U.S. Army Operation IRAQI FREEDOM Study Group report later agreed with Saddam Hussein's assessment on the risk-averse nature of the U.S. military in the 1990s, asserting that "the U.S. military of the 1990s, writ large, had developed a low tolerance both for casualties and for mistakes by tactical commanders." Rayburn and Sobchak, *U.S. Army in the Iraq War*, 21.

THE IRAQI ARMY,1991–1994

The Gulf War significantly degraded, but did not destroy, the Iraqi military. When it invaded Kuwait in 1990, the Iraqi army was the fourth largest in the world with at least 800,000 personnel.[95] U.S. Army estimates put the number as high as 950,000.[96] Coalition forces flew more than 60,000 attack sorties during the Gulf War, targeting Iraqi ground forces, military infrastructure, and the military industrial complex.[97] Captured senior Iraqi officers reported attrition rates for tanks and wheeled vehicles in some Iraqi units as high as 77 percent.[98] By the time of the coalition ground invasion in February 1991, desertion, withdrawal, capture, and combat damage had significantly degraded the enemy forces. According to one estimate, the Iraqi army had abandoned munitions and vehicles for almost three full armored divisions.[99] Before the Gulf War, Iraq had 5,700–6,700 tanks. Of the 3,000 that survived the war, roughly half were the smaller, less powerful T–54s, T–55s, and T–69s, as opposed to the larger, more powerful T–72s and T–62s The Iraqi army emerged from the Gulf War with only 25–33 percent of its prewar military equipment and personnel fully operational, and the coalition's air campaign damaged or destroyed at least 30 percent of Iraq's military industrial complex.[100]

Following the cease-fire, wartime losses and sanctions caused Saddam to reorganize his military. At the beginning of 1992, he inactivated both the *VI* and *VII Corps Headquarters*. The Iraqi army then fielded twenty-nine divisions, down from a high of "seventy or more" during the conflict.[101] Of the remaining divisions, twenty-two were regular army—sixteen infantry, three armored, and three mechanized—and seven *Republican Guard*—three infantry, three armored, and one mechanized. Four *Republican Guard* divisions guarded Baghdad, two defended Mosul, and one Kirkuk. Eleven regular army divisions lined up opposite the Kurdish

95. Cordesman, "Iraq's Military Forces: 1988–1993," 1 Sep 1994, 77.
96. Schubert and Kraus, *Whirlwind War*, 133; Gregory Fontenot, E. J. Degen, and David Tohn, *On Point: The United States Army in Operation Iraqi Freedom* (Fort Leavenworth, KS: Combat Studies Institute Press, 2004), 100.
97. DoD, *Conduct of the Persian Gulf War*, 10 Apr 1992, iii, 198.
98. DoD, *Conduct of the Persian Gulf War*, 10 Apr 1992, 214.
99. Bourque, *Jayhawk!*, 424.
100. For damage to the Iraqi army, see Cordesman, "Iraq's Military Forces: 1988–1993," 1 Sep 1994, 78, 83, 87–88. For damage to Iraq's industry and infrastructure, see DoD, *Conduct of the Persian Gulf War*, 10 Apr 1992, 213.
101. Malovany, *Wars of Modern Babylon*, 605.

province with the other eleven guarding the border with Iran. In 1993, the Iraqi army disbanded four regular army infantry divisions, dropping from twenty-nine to twenty-five divisions overall.[102]

Saddam replaced his military leadership after the Gulf War and the insurrections that followed. He installed a new defense minister, Lt. Gen. Hussein Kamel, who served for six months until Saddam's cousin, Ali Hassan al-Majid, replaced him. Al-Majid's nickname was "Chemical Ali" for his role in the 1988 Halabjah Massacre. Saddam also swapped out his corps commanders. Promotions went to officers who took an active role in suppressing the intifada and to those who dismissed or executed disloyal members of the armed forces. In the process of reorganizing the army's command structure, Saddam purged many officers, but Lt. Gen. Muzahim Sa'ab Hassan remained the Iraqi air force and air defense commander, despite the poor wartime performance of those components.[103]

Despite the austerities of the postwar period, Iraq slowly began to rearm. Limited artillery and ammunition production resumed by March 1992. The following year, Iraq started using resources and spare parts received prior to the Gulf War to repair as many T–72 tanks as possible. Constrained arms production and the inability to purchase modern weaponry from Russia, France, and Italy severely restricted the Iraqi government's capability to modernize its military. However, despite the arms embargo, Iraq was able to purchase T–72 tank parts from Russia and China as well as antitank and antiair missiles from Bulgaria.[104] In the fall of 1994, the Iraqi army's estimated personnel strength was between 350,000 and 400,000.[105] Few Iraqi units approached their prescribed level of strength. Most still suffered from a lack of soldiers and equipment. Although much weaker than before the Gulf War, the Iraqi army—still the largest ground force in the Middle East—posed a threat to its neighboring countries.

---

102. Malovany, *Wars of Modern Babylon*, 605–7.
103. Malovany, *Wars of Modern Babylon*, 600–604.
104. W. Eric Herr, "Operation Vigilant Warrior: Conventional Deterrence Theory, Doctrine, and Practice" (Thesis, U.S. Air Force School of Advanced Air Power Studies, 1996), 11–12; Thomas Sancton, "No Longer Fenced In," *Time*, 23 May 1994.
105. Marine Corps Intel Activity, *Iraq Country Handbook* (Quantico, VA: Marine Corps Intelligence Activity, 1994), 60.

U.S. Central Command began revising its plan for war with Iraq in 1992, the last year of the first Bush administration. The joint planning process for the entire U.S. military moved through a two-year cycle, beginning with the preparation and release of a top secret document called the *Joint Strategic Capabilities Plan.*[106] CENTCOM's new plan for war with Iraq mirrored the one that proved successful in the Gulf War. The 1992 plan focused on the defense of Kuwait—guaranteed by a Defense Cooperation Agreement signed 19 September 1991—and Saudi Arabia, especially the eastern portion with its rich oil fields and production facilities. It called for the same level of forces as had been deployed for Desert Shield and Desert Storm, including two Army corps and a two-division Marine expeditionary force. In the fall of 1992, General Hoar took his chief of war plans, Lt. Col. Richard L. Stouder, to the Pentagon where they briefed Secretary of Defense Cheney, Chairman of the Joint Chiefs of Staff General Colin L. Powell, and Under Secretary of Defense for Policy Paul D. Wolfowitz.

The plan met with a mixed reception. Wolfowitz questioned the large number of ground forces required to execute the plan, noting that the Iraqis had a significantly reduced military capacity since their defeat in the Gulf War two years prior, and that the combination of precision munitions and increased air power in the form of additional Air Force wings would allow the United States to reduce the number and size of proposed ground forces. Stouder later recalled that Wolfowitz's comments "resulted in a spirited discussion, with Gen[eral] Hoar taking the position that the intelligence assessment of Iraqi capability merited a large American ground force and that most of the *Republican Guard* had escaped entirely or with minimal damage."[107] General Powell, whose doctrine included the principle of overwhelming force, sided with General Hoar. "When Wolfowitz saw the discussion going against him he became somewhat prickly," Stouder reported, "and finally Cheney had to step in

---

106. Since the passage of the Goldwater-Nichols Act in 1986, the White House produces a document called the *National Security Strategy*, which the Department of Defense turns into the *National Military Strategy*. The Chairman of the Joint Chiefs of Staff translates the *National Military Strategy* into the *Joint Strategic Capabilities Plan*, which guides the operation plans of the geographic combatant commanders such as the commanding general of U.S. Central Command (CENTCOM).
107. Memoir, Richard L. Stouder, 16 Jun 2007, 1, Historians Files, CMH.

General Powell

forcefully and say, 'That's enough, Paul.'"[108] Apparently, neither Cheney nor his successor officially approved the plan.[109]

Stouder returned to CENTCOM headquarters in Tampa, Florida, to continue the planning process for the next iteration, which would result in an updated product two years later.[110] Third Army planners helped this effort by participating in two planning conferences: one at the U.S. Transportation Command, Scott Air Force Base, Illinois, in April 1993, and the other at CENTCOM in December. The Transportation Command conference produced a deployment plan for the second phase of the operation. The CENTCOM conference adjusted the first forty-five days of the deployment schedule to improve the force flow.[111] However, even as the plan matured, a new National Security Strategy emerged that would soon cause a major shift in war planning for Iraq.

During the first year of his tenure in 1993, President Clinton ordered "a comprehensive review of the nation's defense strategy, force structure, modernization, infrastructure, and foundations" known as the Bottom-Up Review.[112] This study introduced the two-theater strategy—also called the "two major regional conflicts" strategy or the "win-hold-win" strategy—which called upon the United States to prepare to fight two nearly simultaneous wars in different parts of the globe, even while downsizing its military.[113] Lacking the resources to fight two decisive

---

108. Memoir, Stouder, 16 Jun 2007, 1.
109. Col. Roland J. Tiso Jr., Stouder's successor as CENTCOM Chief of War Plans, said that in the fall of 1994, during Operation VIGILANT WARRIOR, "USCENTCOM did not have an approved OPLAN [Operation Plan] 1002, but the aftermath of 'Vigilant Warrior' convinced the Joint Staff and senior leaders that an approved plan was needed." Memoir, Roland J. Tiso Jr., Nov 2019, 1, Historians Files, CMH.
110. This plan became Operation Plan 1002–94, the last stand-alone plan before the requirement for two war plans each for Iraq and North Korea. Interv, J. Travis Moger, CMH, with Richard L. Stouder, 19 Aug 2019, Historians Files, CMH.
111. Annual Historical Review, Third U.S. Army, FY 1993, Exec Sum, 13 Jun 1994, 29.
112. Les Aspin, *Report on the Bottom-Up Review* (Washington, DC: Department of Defense, 1993), iii.
113. In 1998, the term "major regional conflict" was replaced with "major theater war." Memoir, Stephen D. Kidder, "Iraq Planning, 1996–1999," 19 Dec 2019, 2, Historians Files, CMH.

campaigns at the same time, the United States would fight and win in one theater while holding in the other. Then it would shift its forces from the first theater to the second to win there as well. The idea was simple to explain but difficult to translate into a workable plan.

In addition to planning for other contingencies in the Middle East, such as keeping air and sea lines of communications open and possible war with Iran, the CENTCOM planners and their counterparts at the Third Army headquarters now had to create two versions of the war plan for Iraq, depending on whether Iraq would be the first or the second conflict in the two-theater strategy.[114] U.S. Pacific Command (PACOM) faced the same challenge, developing two war plans for North Korea,

Secretary of Defense Cheney
(Department of Defense)

although, to PACOM's advantage, the Clinton administration tended to emphasize the threat from North Korea more than that of an already defeated Iraq. CENTCOM and PACOM each drew up two versions of their major war plans, assuming a forty-five-day gap between the start of each conflict.[115]

The CENTCOM second major contingency plan worried the experts who created it.[116] Both plans generated a detailed list, which laid out the deployment schedules. Although based on available units, the planners questioned whether their own second contingency plan was realistic. Given reductions in the size of the active component and the requirement to prepare for two major near-simultaneous wars, planners relied heavily on the reserve component to fill out their deployment lists. This aspect of the plan did not inspire confidence. Reserve units faced greater readiness, training, and equipment challenges than did their active duty counterparts. They therefore needed longer lead times to become mission capable, particularly in the case of maneuver combat units. This caused

114. For war planning for Iran, see Crist, *Twilight War*, 399, 407–9.
115. At CENTCOM, the primary document was Operation Plan 1002, which planners updated biennially and renumbered as Operation Plan 1003 by early 1997. They initially labeled the second major contingency plan 1003 as well, but later they changed it to 1015. "The 1002 plan was modified and renamed 1003, the first of two MRCs [major regional conflicts], and the former 1003 plan (94 JSCP [Joint Strategic Capabilities Plan] cycle) was renamed 1015, the second of two MRCs." Kidder, "Iraq Planning," 1.
116. Kidder, "Iraq Planning," 1. See also Memoir, Stouder, 16 Jun 2007, 5.

planners to question the wisdom of relying on them for overseas combat operations on short notice.[117] One exasperated planner exclaimed, "That dog ain't gonna hunt!"[118]

A shortage of support units, both active and reserve, further complicated planning efforts. According to Col. Stephen D. Kidder, CENTCOM Chief of War Plans from 1997 to 1999, the shortage was created by the drawdown after the Gulf War and the resulting imbalance in the force. For example, Patriot missile battalions, bridging companies, field hospitals, civil affairs units, and military police were all in short supply.[119] Moreover, the Army could not shift enough support forces from one theater to another, because many of them would be needed throughout a campaign, including posthostilities. This reality caused the chairman of the joint chiefs of staff to include fewer support units than planners recommended in the secondary plan for major regional conflicts, in order to ensure enough assets for each primary contingency.[120] The deficiency led to creative solutions, such as leveraging joint, multinational, and civilian assets to plug gaps wherever possible.[121] Military staffers designated the second plan for Iraq a high risk and an unacceptable risk for North Korea. Nevertheless, they updated the corresponding deployment schedules annually.

The service component headquarters under CENTCOM, including ARCENT, created their own versions of the two plans tailored to their capabilities and missions. Lower echelons assigned to the service components did the same. These efforts resulted in a family of plans all labeled with the same number.

---

117. Ronald E. Sortor, *Army Active/Reserve Mix: Force Planning for Major Regional Contingencies* (Santa Monica, CA: RAND Corporation, 1995), 75.
118. Memoir, Stouder, 16 Jun 2007, 5.
119. Kidder, "War Planning with Missing Pieces," 5.
120. Kidder, "Iraq Planning," 1. See also Kidder, "War Planning with Missing Pieces," 4–5.
121. Kidder, "War Planning with Missing Pieces," 6.

After four years of economic hardship in Iraq, Saddam Hussein was determined to end UN sanctions.[122] The Iraqi president never acknowledged the legality of the sanctions and initially rejected a UN oil-for-food arrangement, which would have allowed Iraq to use some oil revenue to import food, medicine, and other essentials.[123] By 1994, Iraq's economy was in shambles. Prices for consumer goods had skyrocketed and per capita income had fallen drastically, making it difficult for most Iraqis to purchase all but the bare essentials.[124] On 23 September, citing shortages caused by sanctions, the Iraqi government halved daily food rations for the nation's eighteen million people. In just one day, food prices doubled.[125] Medical equipment and drugs were also scarce, causing a crisis in Iraq's already beleaguered healthcare system.

In seeking the termination of sanctions, Saddam's concern was more the survival of his regime than the survival of the Iraqi people. If domestic conditions deteriorated further, Saddam feared that it would cause even more political unrest. An unsuccessful coup in July 1993 and repeated assassination attempts against Saddam underscored the precariousness of his position.[126] Lifting the arms embargo would allow him to equip, arm, and modernize Iraq's military—a critical tool for maintaining internal order and repressing potential dissent. Saddam spent much of 1994 embarked on a so-called charm offensive to undermine UN sanctions, using measured cooperation with UNSCOM and appeals to the international community on behalf of the innocent victims of the sanctions.[127] Taking advantage of a loophole in the UN resolutions, Iraq also negotiated contracts for arms deals and infrastructure projects in anticipation of the lifting of sanctions. Saddam's public relations efforts seemed to be succeeding.

The Iraqi leader had reason to be optimistic about the possible lifting of sanctions. Three permanent members of the UN Security

---

122. S/RES/661.
123. Marr, *Modern History of Iraq*, 239. For the full text of the resolution, see UN Security Council, Resolution 706, Iraq-Kuwait, S/RES/706, 15 Aug 1991, http://unscr. com/en/resolutions/doc/706.
124. Marr, *Modern History of Iraq*, 238. Compare to Sancton, "No Longer Fenced In."
125. Herr, "Operation Vigilant Warrior," 13; Elaine Sciolino, "Kuwait Crisis: Hussein Gambles to Keep Power," *New York Times*, 11 Oct 1994.
126. Marr, *Modern History of Iraq*, 241; Sciolino, "Kuwait Crisis."
127. Herr, "Operation Vigilant Warrior," 14.

Council—France, Russia, and China—all wanted to end the sanctions regime. All three countries had a history of selling arms to Iraq and stood to gain lucrative contracts for rebuilding the country. Iraq had accumulated large debts to both France and Russia—$6 billion and $5 billion, respectively—during the Iran-Iraq War.[128] An end to the oil embargo would give Baghdad the capital to buy arms and pay its debts. The United States and Great Britain, however, adamantly opposed the lifting of sanctions until Iraq complied with all UN resolutions, including the complete dismantling of its WMD program.

At the same time as these rising tensions with Iraq, an ongoing crisis reached a breaking point in the Caribbean nation of Haiti. In September 1991, Lt. Gen. J. Raoul Cédras had ousted President Jean-Bertrand Aristide, a former Roman Catholic priest and Haiti's democratically elected head of state. As with Iraq, the UN imposed economic sanctions to pressure the Cédras government. Because of a combination of political repression and extreme poverty, thousands of refugees fled the country in small vessels bound for the United States.[129] In July 1994, after nearly three years of failed UN efforts to get Cédras to leave, the UN Security Council authorized "all necessary means" to remove Cédras's military junta from power and restore Haiti's legitimate government.[130]

The United States took the lead with Operation UPHOLD DEMOCRACY and prepared for two contingencies: one for a forcible entry and another for a permissive entry should last-minute diplomacy prove fruitful. When Cédras agreed to a transition under threat of a hostile invasion, units designated for the forcible-entry option, already en route to Haiti, returned to their bases. The permissive entry force arrived in Haiti on 19 September to preserve civil order, protect the interests of American citizens and third-country nationals, and restore the Aristide government. U.S. Army strength in UPHOLD DEMOCRACY peaked at more than 18,000 in October 1994.[131]

The same month the United States deployed troops to Haiti, Saddam increased his antisanctions rhetoric ahead of the next UNSCOM report

---

128. Herr, "Operation Vigilant Warrior," 13–14.
129. As part of Operation SEA SIGNAL (August 1994–February 1996), the U.S. government housed Haitian migrants rescued at sea in temporary facilities at the Guantanamo Bay Naval Base, Cuba. "At the height of Operation SEA SIGNAL in FY 1995, the migrant population reached 21,638 Haitian and 32,780 Cuban migrants." Stephen L. Y. Gammons and William M. Donnelly, *DAHSUM, FY 1995* (Washington, DC: U.S. Army Center of Military History, 2004), 46–47.
130. UN Security Council, Resolution 940, Authorization to Form a Multinational Force under Unified Command and Control to Restore the Legitimately Elected President and Authorities of the Government of Haiti and Extension of the Mandate of the UN Mission in Haiti, S/RES/940, 31 Jul 1994, http://unscr.com/en/resolutions/doc/940.
131. Richard W. Stewart, ed., *American Military History*, vol. 2, *The United States Army in a Global Era, 1917–2008*, Army Historical Series, 2nd ed. (Washington, DC: U.S. Army Center of Military History, 2010), 437–40; Brown, *Kevlar Legions*, 114–15. For troop strength in Haiti, see Gammons and Donnelly, *DAHSUM, FY 1995*, 46.

to the UN Security Council, due on 10 October. Although UNSCOM Chairman C. Rolf Ekéus doubted Iraq had come clean about its biological weapons program, he was satisfied that UNSCOM had largely achieved its goals in identifying and dismantling Iraq's chemical and missile programs.[132] In light of this progress, the commission was shifting its focus to monitoring compliance. U.S. intelligence officials, however, had even greater concerns about Iraq's WMD capabilities and intentions. CIA Director R. James Woolsey Jr. announced that Iraq had hidden some weapons programs, was building underground facilities to resume these programs, and harbored ambitions of seizing Kuwait again. On 25 September, an Iraqi government official stated that Baghdad would reconsider its cooperation with the weapons inspectors if the UN did not ease or lift sanctions. In this tense environment, Ekéus visited Iraq during the first week of October to discuss ongoing monitoring of suspected WMD sites.

On 4 October, while Ekéus was in Baghdad, a British GR–1 Tornado, flying a SOUTHERN WATCH reconnaissance mission, photographed an Iraqi transport on the highway between Qal'at Salih and Al Basrah. An initial photographic analysis in Dhahran, Saudi Arabia, concluded that it was headed north and carrying an older T–55 tank. When intelligence analysts in Riyadh took another look at the images, they determined that the vehicle was actually carrying a modern T–72 tank and heading south. This was the first solid indication of an Iraqi troop movement. Over the next two days, U.S. intelligence analysts scoured the available imagery to determine which Iraqi units were moving and where. They determined that two *Republican Guard* divisions—the *Hammurabi* and *Al-Nida*—were moving south to the Iraqi *III Corps* area near Al Basrah. On 6 October, CENTCOM received a "national warning message" about the Iraqi deployments.[133] (*See Map 6.*) Alongside the three regular army divisions permanently stationed in the south, the arrival of two *Republican Guard* formations would give Saddam five heavy divisions within striking distance of Kuwait.[134] The Iraqi positions, including a forward command post at Az Zubayr, resembled those just before the 1990 invasion of Kuwait.[135]

Baghdad's rhetoric became ominous as Iraqi troops continued to move toward the border. The same day CENTCOM learned of the Iraqi *Republican Guard* deployments, Iraq's Deputy Prime Minister Tariq Aziz demanded that UNSCOM set a date for lifting sanctions and made a veiled threat about Iraq looking for other means to defend itself.[136] This

---

132. Sancton, "No Longer Fenced In."

133. Stanley A. Puckett and Jay E. Hines, "The October Surprise: Operation Vigilant Warrior, 10 October – 22 December 1994" (Unpublished Rpt, n.d.), 27, General Peay Collection, U.S. Army Heritage and Education Center, Carlisle, PA.

134. Frank Williams, "The Projection of Force: Two Weeks in the Life of Third United States Army" (Unpublished Rpt, Jun 2015), ch. 1, 6, Opn VIGILANT WARRIOR Collection, CMH.

135. Puckett and Hines, "October Surprise," 32.

136. Puckett and Hines, "October Surprise," 18.

kind of saber-rattling was nothing new. Saddam had made similar threats that March. However, the combination of threats and troop movements set off alarm bells in Washington that soon reverberated at CENTCOM headquarters in Tampa. General Peay, who had assumed command in August that year, received a briefing about unusual troop movements in southern Iraq. Lead elements were only 50 kilometers from the Kuwaiti border, and at the current rate of movement, four *Republican Guard* brigades could be on the border by 10 October.[137] This was also the date scheduled for the next sixty-day review of Iraq's compliance with UN resolutions and Saddam's deadline for a commitment from the UN Security Council on the lifting of sanctions.[138]

At the time, the U.S.-led coalition had insufficient aircraft to deter an Iraqi ground assault, much less launch a counterattack. A substantial number of Air Force and British Royal Air Force (RAF) assets in the region enforced the no-fly zone below the 32nd parallel, but these aircraft were not equipped to stop advancing armored divisions.[139] In the first week of October, JTF SWA had only eighteen F–16C Falcons and six British GR–1 Tornados to oppose the Iraqi divisions moving south.[140] Moreover, no forward air controllers, liaison officers, and other personnel were in the theater to conduct extensive close air support operations. The Kuwaiti air force had twenty-four new F–18s, but it is unclear if the fighters and their crews were combat ready.

The United States and Kuwait had minimal ground forces in the region. Kuwait fielded four understrength brigades—two armored, one mechanized infantry, and one motorized cavalry—with a total of approximately 12,000 soldiers, plus a unit with a single antiarmor helicopter.[141] CENTCOM also had limited forces in the country. Camp Doha, the Army's only permanent base in the emirate, consisted of roughly 180 Army personnel, a detachment of approximately 300 soldiers from the 513th Military Intelligence Brigade, and some 1,200 civilian contractors.[142] The command's primary responsibility was to

---

137. Puckett and Hines, "October Surprise," 24.
138. Puckett and Hines, "October Surprise," A-137.
139. Daniel L. Byman and Matthew C. Waxman, *Confronting Iraq: U.S. Policy and the Use of Force Since the Gulf War* (Santa Monica, CA: RAND Corporation, 2000), 55. W. Eric Herr, a U.S. Air Force officer, wrote, "There were 9 F–15C, 24 F–16C, 12 Allied fighters, and 29 fixed wing support aircraft in theater on 9 October 1994." He goes on to say, "There was substantial coalition air presence in the area of responsibility (AOR), but it was there as a part of Operation SOUTHERN WATCH. The aircraft were enforcing the no-fly zone south of the 32nd parallel, and were not outfitted to stop an armor advance." Herr did not specify what this meant. Herr, "Operation Vigilant Warrior," 26–27, 27n7.
140. Puckett and Hines, "October Surprise," 37–38.
141. Williams, "Projection of Force," ch. 1, 10; ch. 2, 3–4. Compare to Herr, "Operation Vigilant Warrior," 26.
142. Williams, "Projection of Force," ch. 1, 9. At the time, the Army garrison at Camp Doha appeared in some source literature as Area Support Group–Kuwait, but this may not have been an official unit name. For more on the unit name, see page 45.

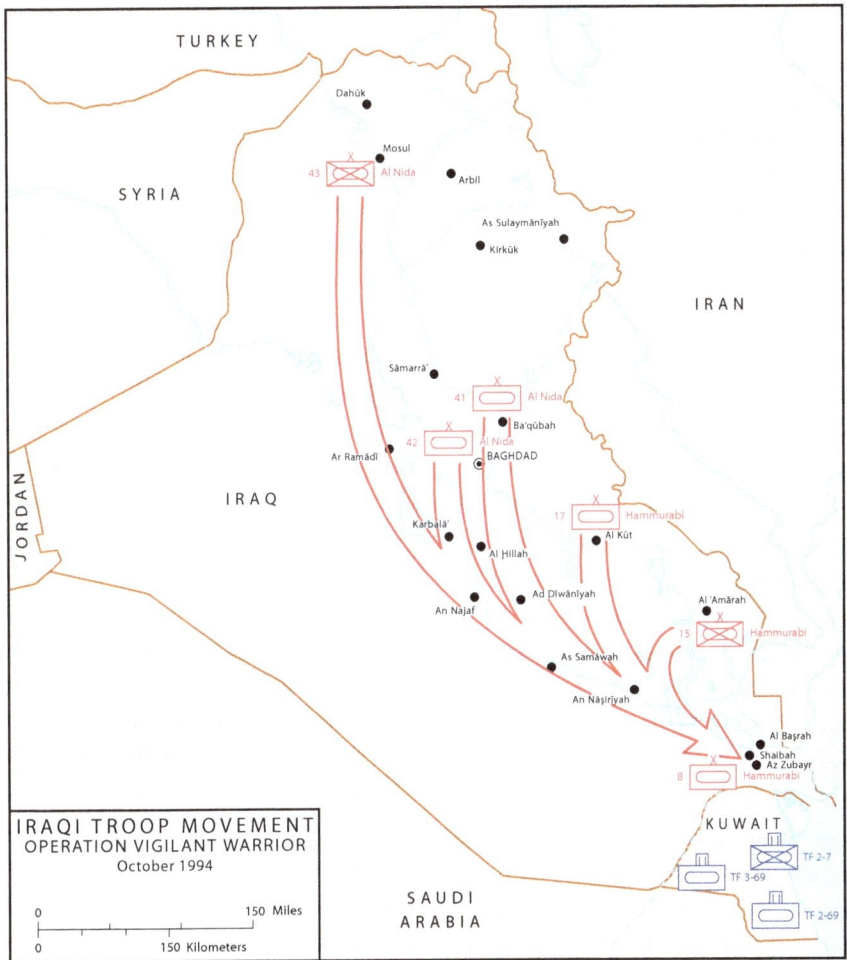

Map showing Iraq with surrounding countries (TURKEY, SYRIA, JORDAN, SAUDI ARABIA, IRAN, KUWAIT) and Iraqi troop movements.

Map labels include: Dahūk, Mosul, Al Nida, Arbil, As Sulaymānīyah, Kirkūk, Sāmarrā', Al Nida, Ba'qūbah, Al Nida, BAGHDAD, Ar Ramādī, Karbalā', Al Hillah, Hammurabi, Al Kūt, An Najaf, Ad Dīwānīyah, Al 'Amārah, As Samāwah, Hammurabi, An Nāşirīyah, Al Başrah, Shaibah, Az Zubayr, Hammurabi, KUWAIT, TF 2-7, TF 3-69, TF 2-69, SAUDI ARABIA

IRAQI TROOP MOVEMENT
OPERATION VIGILANT WARRIOR
October 1994

0 — 150 Miles
0 — 150 Kilometers

Map 6

maintain AWR-5, stored at Camp Doha and used by the battalions that deployed for INTRINSIC ACTION training exercises. The next INTRINSIC ACTION rotation was scheduled to begin mid-October, so the designated units from the 1st Infantry Division were still at their home station, Fort Riley, Kansas.[143] As it happened, the only U.S. combat troops in Kuwait at the time were sixty-five Special Forces soldiers from Company C, 2d Battalion, 5th Special Forces Group, 1st Special Forces, who had arrived on 3 October for an IRIS GOLD training exercise with the Kuwaiti military. Not only were there too few troops, but pre-positioned stocks also came up short. AWR-5 was supposed to outfit a brigade; however, not all of the allocated equipment had arrived from recently inactivated VII Corps

---

143. Williams, "Projection of Force," ch. 1, 15.

units in Europe.[144] The limited personnel strength and materiel meant that coalition ground forces were insufficient to halt the advancing Iraqi *Republican Guard* divisions without significant reinforcements.[145]

The maritime assets in the theater, however, were more extensive. Although the Navy had no carrier in the Persian Gulf, five major combat ships armed with Tomahawk cruise missiles were present. The USS *Tripoli* Amphibious Ready Group was also in the Gulf. Its landing force, the 15th Marine Expeditionary Unit—an air-ground task force centered on an infantry battalion—had approximately 2,000 marines ashore in the United Arab Emirates conducting exercises.[146]

As the United States began making plans to deter Saddam's forces, the Iraqi troop movements continued. On Friday, 7 October, the *Hammurabi Division*'s *15th Mechanized Brigade* and *17th Armored Brigade* were at Shaibah Air Base, a former RAF facility approximately 28 kilometers from the border, near the town of Az Zubayr.[147] The *Al-Nida Division*'s *43d Mechanized Brigade* was embarking on rail cars in Mosul. At the current rates of movement, CENTCOM estimated that the *Republican Guard* would have six brigades—two full divisions—in the south by 13 October.[148]

Given the limited number of friendly combat-ready forces in the region, the priority for General Peay was to send as many coalition forces to Kuwait as quickly as possible. He telephoned his subordinate commanders to stress the urgency of the situation. "SECDEF [the secretary of defense] feels it's serious," he told Lt. Gen. Steven L. Arnold, now the commander of the Third Army. Peay informed Arnold that Air Force Maj. Gen. Everett H. Pratt Jr., the commander of JTF SWA in Riyadh, would run operations in the theater until the arrival of CENTCOM's deputy commander in chief, General Neal. Peay ordered Arnold to send a senior commander from the Third Army to Kuwait. Arnold chose his deputy, Maj. Gen. James B. Taylor. The CINCCENT stressed the importance of moving heavy ground forces to the Gulf quickly to "stop this guy."[149]

After speaking with Arnold, Peay wondered aloud to his staff whether General Taylor would be able to defend against a possible Iraqi attack with the limited resources available. "Will General Taylor

---

144. Williams, "Projection of Force," ch. 1, 9.

145. The fact that the Kuwaiti government requested U.S. ground troops to reinforce their brigades suggests that they did not believe their own military would be capable of defending the country against the threat.

146. Herr, "Operation Vigilant Warrior," 27.

147. During World War I, the British Army fought and won a considerable victory over Ottoman forces in the area at the Battle of Shaibah, 12–14 April 1915. Michael Crawshaw, *The First World War Battlefield Guide*, vol. 2, *The Forgotten Fronts* (Andover, UK: British Army Headquarters, 2016), 76.

148. Puckett and Hines, "October Surprise," 26.

149. Notes, General J. H. Binford Peay III, 6 Oct–9 Dec 1994, "XO's Notes," 2–3, General Peay Collection, U.S. Army Heritage and Education Center, Carlisle, PA.

stand and fight or go south?" he asked.[150] Peay's question was one of tactics, not courage, and it highlighted the precariousness of the situation. The same day, Peay stood up his Crisis Action Team. He also requested the immediate deployment of Air Force and Navy assets to the Gulf: KC–130 tankers, U–2 and RC–135 reconnaissance aircraft, and the USS *George Washington* Carrier Battle Group. At a 1700 update with his staff, Peay again raised the possibility of evacuating Camp Doha: "At some point do we want to retrograde [AWR-5] equipment south? We have a 3–5 day vulnerable window."[151]

The Kuwaitis also took the threat seriously. On 7 October, Peay learned that Ambassador Ryan C. Crocker had relayed a request from

General Arnold

the government of Kuwait for ground troops, a Patriot missile battery, and a statement of U.S. intentions. To reassure the Kuwaitis and meet the immediate threat, General Peay requested from Washington the deployment of a "3x3 battalion task force"—three mechanized and three armored companies.[152] That evening, the Kuwaiti Land Forces headquarters deployed all four of its brigades into defensive positions in the desert northwest of Kuwait City.

However, leaders at Camp Doha did not sense the same urgency as in Washington, Tampa, Atlanta, or the rest of Kuwait. Even as the Kuwaitis stocked up on groceries and queued at gas stations, the Camp Doha commander, Col. Robert L. Smalser, went ahead with a planned 8 October unit picnic, which Ambassador Crocker also attended.[153] Later, Smalser recalled that he did not believe the Iraqi Army had the ability to attack successfully. As he saw it, they had neither the necessary command and control capability nor sufficient support in place.[154] This assessment, which contradicted CENTCOM's, was based on limited intelligence, because the 513th Military Intelligence detachment did not have access to CENTCOM's satellite imagery until 1995.[155] Nevertheless, on the day of the

---

150. Peay, "XO's Notes," 4.
151. Peay, "XO's Notes," 8.
152. Peay, "XO's Notes," 5.
153. Williams, "Projection of Force," ch. 1, 26–27.
154. Williams, "Projection of Force," ch. 1, 27.
155. Williams, "Projection of Force," ch. 1, 5. On 8 October 1994, CENTCOM's director

67

picnic, U.S. Special Forces soldiers were embedded with their coalition partners in the desert northwest of Kuwait City, preparing for a seemingly imminent Iraqi offensive.

Kuwait was not alone in its mobilization of forces. President Clinton ordered "the USS *George Washington* Carrier Battle Group, cruise missile ships, a Marine Expeditionary Brigade, and an Army mechanized task force" to the Persian Gulf.[156] Speaking to reporters as he left the White House for Camp David, the president said, "I want to make it clear one more time, it would be a grave error for Iraq to repeat the mistakes of the past or to misjudge either American will or American power."[157]

Once the president issued a deployment order, lead units moved quickly in response to CENTCOM's request for forces. Two Patriot missile batteries of the 2d Battalion,

General Taylor (*center*) speaks with a soldier at Tactical Assembly Area LIBERTY outside Kuwait City.
(*National Archives*)

43d Air Defense Artillery, arrived in Saudi Arabia on 8 October: one in Riyadh, the other in Dhahran. The plan was for them to drive their equipment to Kuwait.[158] The same day, the Army ordered elements of the 7th Transportation Group to Kuwait and Saudi Arabia. The Third Army forward headquarters left Georgia on 8 October. When Taylor flew to Kuwait to establish Joint Task Force–Kuwait (JTF-Kuwait), Arnold did not have a written mission, which Third Army planners were still developing, to give to his deputy. Working in three locations on two continents during a rapidly evolving crisis complicated the planning efforts.[159] While staffers raced to develop formal guidance, Arnold issued

---

of intelligence, Brig. Gen. James C. King, told General Peay that Saddam had both the capability and the intent to attack into Kuwait and threaten Kuwait City, but could not do the same to Saudi Arabia. Peay, "XO's Notes," 10.

156. William J. Clinton, *Public Papers of the Presidents of the United States: William J. Clinton, 1994, Book 1* (Washington, DC: Government Printing Office, 1995), 1726. The president was summarizing deployments made over the previous weekend.

157. Clinton, *Public Papers of the Presidents of the United States: William J. Clinton, 1994, Book 1*, 1725.

158. Peay, "XO's Notes," 5. For more on air defense artillery deployments throughout the 1990s, see Kirkpatrick, *"Ruck It Up!,"* 345–85.

159. According to the after action report, "the rapid developing crisis of Operation VIGILANT WARRIOR highlighted the need for a comprehensive operations plan for the

verbal orders based on discussions with General Peay. In addition to setting up JTF-Kuwait, Taylor was to assess the Kuwaiti defenses and take command of U.S. ground forces.[160] Upon arrival on Sunday, 9 October, the general and his staff converted a warehouse at Camp Doha into a command post, where they worked around the clock for the next forty-eight hours. Lacking time to deploy the Third Army's "Lucky TAC" mobile command post, Taylor improvised.[161] As the Army forces landed in Kuwait and Saudi Arabia, Navy ships sailed toward the Persian Gulf. In addition to the USS *George Washington* Carrier Battle Group, which was already heading from the Adriatic toward the Red Sea, on 9 October the Navy deployed five ships carrying AWR-3 from Diego Garcia in the Indian Ocean to the Port of Dammam, Saudi Arabia.

As units headed to the Middle East during the first weekend of the crisis, Arnold's staff, in coordination with CENTCOM planners, crafted a mission statement: "Third Army would deploy forces to theater, deter an Iraqi attack, defend Kuwait if necessary to protect critical coalition assets, and be prepared to counterattack and conduct offensive operations."[162] This expansive statement reflected the ambiguity surrounding Saddam's intentions. It remained unclear whether the deployment of *Republican Guard* troops to the border was simply a show of force or a prelude to another invasion of Kuwait. The absence of human intelligence from inside Iraq forced the intelligence community to rely on interpretations of Saddam's past behavior. On that basis, analysts generally assumed hostile intent.[163] U.S. military planners had this mindset as they began developing a contingency plan.

As the planners refined their deployment schedule, Iraq's forces continued to move south. By 9 October, all three brigades of the *Hammurabi Division* were already in southern Iraq. Two brigades—the *15th Mechanized* and *17th Armored*—were at Shaibah; the *8th Armored Brigade* was a little farther south, just 15 kilometers from the Kuwait border. All three brigades of the *Al-Nida Division* were heading south by rail from their bases in northern Iraq and lead elements were already in Shaibah. An armored battalion from a third *Republican Guard* division was moving from Qal'at Salih, north of Al Basrah, toward Shaibah. CENTCOM analysts determined that both the *Hammurabi Division* and the *Al-Nida Division* would have massed near the border by 13 October, enabling Iraq to launch

defense of Kuwait. To meet this challenge, planning started in Kuwait by TF–Kuwait [JTF-Kuwait], in Atlanta by ARCENT–REAR, and in Riyadh by ARCENT–Main." AAR, Joint Uniform Lessons Learned System Long Rpt (JULLS #12522–14156), U.S. Army Central, 4 Dec 1994, sub: Operation VIGILANT WARRIOR conducted by ARCENT on 10/12/94, 1, Historians Files, CMH.
160. Williams, "Projection of Force," ch. 1, 14.
161. Williams, "Projection of Force," ch. 2, 5n4.
162. Williams, "Projection of Force," ch. 1, 20.
163. Michael A. Knights, *Cradle of Conflict: Iraq and the Birth of Modern U.S. Military Power* (Annapolis, MD: Naval Institute Press, 2005), 146.

a five-division attack with *Republican Guard* and regular army divisions already in the area.[164]

Maj. Gen. Joseph E. DeFrancisco's 24th Infantry Division (Mechanized) worked around the clock to deploy its units to meet the threat. DeFrancisco ordered 2d Battalion, 7th Infantry (Mechanized), organized as Task Force 2–7, to deploy first. This battalion had just completed an INTRINSIC ACTION exercise, so its members were familiar with the pre-positioned equipment, the terrain, and the Kuwaiti military. After receiving an unofficial warning order on 7 October and the official notification the following day, two Task Force 2–7 companies—one armor and one mechanized—plus a battalion headquarters element were ready to fly out by noon on 9 October. They landed in Kuwait on the evening of 10 October. After drawing their equipment and ammunition at Camp Doha, the two companies were in their tactical assembly area within forty-eight hours. Lead elements of their sister battalion—3d Battalion, 69th Armor, organized as Task Force 3–69—reached Kuwait on 11 October. The rest of the two battalions continued to arrive over the next few days.

The deployment of troops did not always go as planned. S. Sgt. Andrew Conrad, who was on the Task Force 2–7 advance party, flew out of Savannah, Georgia, on 10 October but did not arrive in Kuwait until 14 October because his C–5 aircraft "kept breaking down."[165] Many such glitches occurred during the rapid deployment phase.

As the first American warfighting units were in the air on their way to Kuwait, the United States and its allies approved more deployments. On 10 October, General John M. D. Shalikashvili, now Chairman of the Joint Chiefs of Staff, issued an execution order for Operation VIGILANT WARRIOR. General Peay subsequently requested an additional 374 fixed-wing aircraft. To prepare for a possible full-scale Iraqi invasion of Kuwait, Peay also asked for three full Army divisions—the 1st Infantry Division, the 24th Infantry Division (Mechanized), and the 101st Airborne Division (Air Assault)—and the III Corps headquarters to provide command and control. The joint staff alerted these units, which began making preparations to deploy.[166] The United Kingdom also announced it was sending 4,000 Royal Marines and an additional six Tornados.[167] The British also promised two ships: the frigate HMS *Cornwall* and the destroyer HMS *Cardiff*. France committed the frigate *Georges Leygues*.[168]

Just as the coalition began taking shape, the Iraqis changed course. After the first 300 soldiers from Task Force 2–7 arrived in Kuwait, the Iraqi ambassador to the United Nations, Nizar Hamdoon, announced

164. Puckett and Hines, "October Surprise," 42.
165. Interv, Maj. Michael W. Byrne with soldiers from Co A, 2d Bn, 7th Inf (Mech), 28 Nov 1994, CMH Catalog No. VWIT–A–027b, Opn VIGILANT WARRIOR Collection, CMH.
166. Peay, "XO's Notes," 4, 22.
167. Puckett and Hines, "October Surprise," 43–44.
168. Herr, "Operation Vigilant Warrior," 28.

that Iraqi troops were "already on the move" to a site north of Al Basrah.[169] Iraqi Foreign Minister Mohammed Saeed al-Sahhaf added that the troops would redeploy to "other locations in the rear" to complete military exercises.[170]

President Clinton addressed the nation from the White House Oval Office at 2000. After outlining the progress in ongoing operations in Haiti, the president discussed military deployments to the Persian Gulf: "Today I have ordered the additional deployment of 350 Air Force aircraft to the region." He added, "Iraq announced today that it will pull back its troops from the Kuwait border. But we're interested in facts, not promises, in deeds, not words. And we have not yet seen evidence that Iraq's troops are in fact pulling back. We'll be watching very closely to see if they do so."[171]

In fact, reconnaissance imagery showed no signs that the Iraqi *Republican Guard* divisions were moving north. A British Tornado pho-

General DeFrancisco as a brigadier general

tographed more than one hundred Iraqi T–72 tanks near the demilitarized zone.[172] Peay told his subordinate commanders to disregard news reports of Iraq pulling back. In agreement with Peay, Arnold said that he was not going to take the bait and told his staff to ignore what they heard in the American news.[173]

The generals had good reason to be skeptical, based not only on intelligence reports but also on historical precedents. Iraq had perfected the art of deception during the Iran-Iraq War. After the Iraqis invaded Kuwait in 1990, they made false withdrawal announcements, which they used to buy time to reposition their forces. When the ground war began in February 1991, the Iraqis had announced their

169. Puckett and Hines, "October Surprise," 47; Mark Matthews, "U.S. Sees No Iraqi Pullback, Beefs Up Airpower," *Baltimore Sun*, 11 Oct 1994, http://www.baltimoresun.com/news/bs-xpm-1994-10-11-1994284091-story.html.
170. Puckett and Hines, "October Surprise," 47; "Iraq Says It's Ending Border Build-Up," *St. Louis Post-Dispatch*, 11 Oct 1994, http://www.questia.com/newspaper/1P2-32899447/iraq-says-it-s-ending-border-buildup. Sahhaf would earn the moniker "Baghdad Bob" for his overly optimistic televised assessments of Iraq's performance during the 2003 Iraq War.
171. Clinton, *Public Papers of the Presidents of the United States: William J. Clinton*, 1994, Book 1, 1726.
172. Puckett and Hines, "October Surprise," 47.
173. Williams, "Projection of Force," ch. 2, 5.

plans to remove their forces from Kuwait, but the coalition forces saw no signs of withdrawal.

Consequently, the United States and Great Britain continued to send forces to the Gulf. Even when Western intelligence agencies observed Iraqi *Republican Guard* units moving north again, senior American military officers suspected it might be a feint. On 13 October, General Peay told NBC's *Today Show* that "the crisis is not past. . . . We have diffused the crisis but we will have to watch the situation closely."[174] Peay's suspicions seemed warranted when the *Al-Nida Division* halted its northward movement at An Nasiriyah on the Euphrates about 200 kilometers northwest of Al Basrah. This raised the possibility that the withdrawal was a deception intended to stop the movement of coalition forces to the region. However, the Defense Intelligence Agency concluded that the *Al-Nida Division*'s halt at An Nasiriyah was likely because of transportation problems.[175] Both Peay and Shalikashvili still thought it prudent to send a second brigade.

A debate ensued over whether to deploy the 3d Brigade, 24th Infantry Division, to Saudi Arabia as planned. Peay wanted the unit to reinforce the theater, but Army leaders were concerned that deploying another brigade would be too expensive, especially with the Iraqi threat appearing to diminish. Accordingly, eight planeloads of 7th Transportation Group personnel bound for Dhahran turned around midflight over the Atlantic Ocean, because the transportation unit's role was to support the 3d Brigade. However, General Shalikashvili did not want to send a premature message that the crisis was over. To underscore the American commitment to regional security and reduce the likelihood that Saddam would reverse his withdrawal decision, the chairman told Peay to deploy a second heavy brigade.[176] This order required the eight rerouted aircraft to turn around again, proceed to their original destinations, and prepare for the arrival of the 3d Brigade. These rapid shifts in deployment plans attested to the general uncertainty about Saddam's intentions and objectives.

While CENTCOM continued to send military forces into theater, diplomats worked to prevent a repeat of Saddam's provocative and unexpected troop deployment. Technically, Iraq's movement of divisions to the Kuwait border had not violated existing UN resolutions. In light of this, U.S. diplomats sought a new restriction on such troop movements. U.S. Ambassador to the United Nations Madeleine J. K. Albright explained, "What we're looking at are ways to try to make sure that they stay well, well behind their borders."[177] As a result of these efforts, the UN Security Council unanimously passed Resolution 949 on 15 October,

174. Quoted in Herr, "Operation Vigilant Warrior," 31.
175. Puckett and Hines, "October Surprise," 52.
176. Williams, "Projection of Force," ch. 2, 8; J. H. Binford Peay III, "The Five Pillars of Peace in the Central Region," *Joint Forces Quarterly* (Autumn 1995): 32.
177. Quoted in Bradley Graham and Ruth Marcus, "Administration Plans More Limits on Iraq," *Washington Post*, 12 Oct 1994.

demanding that "Iraq immediately complete the withdrawal of all military units recently deployed to southern Iraq to their original positions."[178] Iraq quickly acceded to the Security Council's demand. The UN also ordered that Iraq not "take any other action to enhance its military capacity in southern Iraq."[179] To enforce this order, the United States and its allies created a ground exclusion zone south of the 32nd parallel—a "no-drive zone" that functioned as a corollary to the no-fly zone.

In the second week of the crisis, the operational focus shifted as the threat of an Iraqi attack subsided. By 15 October, one week after President Clinton had given the deployment order, the first two battalions from the requested 3x3 battalion task force were in Kuwait. By 17 October, they had drawn their equipment and ammunition at Camp Doha and were in the desert northwest of the capital ready to support the Kuwaiti army.[180] However, this was still a thin screen against the available Iraqi forces in southern Iraq (approximately 50,000 regular army troops in Al Basrah and the *Republican Guard* division at An Nasiriyah) should they attack. That possibility seemed remote after the *Al-Nida Division* started moving north again on 18 October. The president canceled the deployment of 18,000 marines from the I Marine Expeditionary Force and released 156,000 other personnel who were on alert. The crisis appeared to be over.

Although still officially a contingency operation, VIGILANT WARRIOR evolved into a training exercise, and deployments slowed accordingly. On 17 October, Task Force 2–69, composed of elements from the 2d Battalion, 69th Armor, assembled in Ad Dammam, Saudi Arabia. The unit stayed for several days in a hangar at Lucky Base, the ARCENT facility about 30 kilometers from the port, waiting to get their equipment from AWR-3 before moving north to Kuwait. By the time the first two Military Sealift Command roll-on/roll-off ships—MV *Cape Horn* and MV *Cape Decision*—were ready to offload cargo on 22 October, the crisis with Iraq had passed. Also on this day, elements of the 1st Battalion, 18th Infantry, from the 3d Brigade, 24th Infantry Division—the core of Task Force 1–18—began to trickle into Ad Dammam in time for its Companies A and B to join Task Force 2–69 on the trip north a few days later.

The soldiers found the tanks in excellent condition, but none of their batteries worked because they had neither been properly maintained nor checked prior to offloading.[181] Every vehicle had to be jumpstarted in order

---

178. UN Security Council, Resolution 949, Demanding that Iraq Immediately Complete the Withdrawal of All Military Units Recently Deployed to Southern Iraq to Their Original Positions and that Iraq Not Again Utilize its Military or Any Other Forces in a Hostile or Provocative Manner to Threaten its Neighbours, S/RES/949, 15 Oct 1994, http://unscr.com/en/resolutions/doc/949.

179. S/RES/949.

180. AAR, 24th Inf Div (Mech), 24 Nov 1994, Opn VIGILANT WARRIOR Collection, CMH.

181. AAR, 6th Transportation Bn (Truck), 10 Jan 1995, U.S. Army History and Education Center, Carlisle, PA.

to be moved down the ramp and onto the pier, slowing the operation.[182] Eventually, the AMC cargo specialists, working with 6th Transportation Battalion and 3d Brigade soldiers, finished unloading the tanks, trucks, and other equipment. Soldiers then moved everything to an assembly area to prepare for convoy operations.

U.S. troops encountered myriad difficulties throughout the exercise, not just at the port. The onward movement from Ad Dammam, Saudi Arabia, to the tactical assembly area in northern Kuwait took place over three days from 26 to 28 October. Owing to a lack of drivers and equipment, the 6th Transportation Battalion, commanded by Lt. Col. Kathleen M. Gainey, augmented their capacity with drivers and vehicles supplied by the Saudi army and by contractors. Inferior

Colonel Gainey
(Courtesy of Lt. Gen. [Ret.] Kathleen M. Gainey)

foreign equipment combined with language and culture barriers caused numerous problems. Few Arabic interpreters were available, which made it difficult to communicate with Saudi drivers. The Saudi soldiers refused to eat the Army's packaged meals and said they would bring and cook their own food. The 6th Transportation Battalion after action report relates what happened next: "The Saudis did bring food with them but not the kind of food we expected. They traveled with live goats and propane stoves and expected to have time to slaughter and cook their meal when we stopped."[183] Once the convoys got under way, Saudi drivers did not maintain convoy integrity and kept speeding and passing each other. Consequently, more tires blew out and more vehicles broke down than what the Americans expected. When the convoy stopped to rest and refuel, the Saudis did not get back in their vehicles when it was time for the convoy to proceed. Loud arguments between the drivers and their superiors ensued. "The Saudis were not used to working the length of time we expected them to," the after action report explained. The situation improved once the convoys crossed the border, where Kuwaiti police escorts slowed the pace and kept Saudi drivers in line with orders

---

182. Interv, Maj. Michael W. Byrne with Capt. Donald V. Phillips, Co Cdr, Co A, 2d Bn, 69th Armor, 3d Bde, 24th Inf Div (Mech), 9 Nov 1994, CMH Catalog No. VWIT–A–007b, Opn Vigilant Warrior Collection, CMH.
183. AAR, 6th Transportation Bn (Truck), 10 Jan 1995.

A U.S. Army stevedore directs an M1A1 Abrams tank down the ramp of the Ready Reserve Force ship MV *Cape Decision.*

(*National Archives*)

barked over their loudspeakers.[184] Despite these problems, the coalition partners and their equipment enabled the 6th Transportation Battalion to move a total of 376 pieces of equipment to Kuwait in three days.

The Army had hurried to the Middle East to fight but wound up training instead. Once 3d Brigade units arrived in their tactical assembly area northwest of Kuwait City, they joined the 1st Brigade, 24th Infantry Division, for live-fire exercises to practice counterattacking along a designated approach to a firing position. When the 3d Brigade's armored task force (Task Force 2–69) had completed the training, it withdrew to Saudi Arabia to a facility near the Port of Dammam. The 3d Brigade soldiers cleaned their equipment and turned it in. With input from the 24th Infantry Division, AMC personnel created a new load plan for maximum efficiency and put the equipment on the Military Sealift Command ships for transport back to Diego Garcia.[185]

During Vigilant Warrior, the Navy did more than just provide sealift for Army equipment; it enforced UN sanctions against Iraq by interdicting smugglers. On 22 October, a U.S. Navy warship in the Persian Gulf stopped the Honduran-flagged oil tanker *Al Mahrousa.* After boarding, Navy and Coast Guard personnel found that the vessel's paperwork was not in order. The ship's Egyptian master admitted to loading 3,162 tons of diesel fuel in Iraq, then sailing into international waters in violation of the four-year-old oil embargo. His contractor told him to sail to Sirri, an Iranian island off the coast of Dubai, to await instructions on where to deliver his contraband cargo. The Navy turned

---

184. Interv, Byrne with Phillips, 9 Nov 1994.
185. Interv, Byrne with Phillips, 9 Nov 1994.

A convoy from the 2d Battalion, 69th Armor, carries material needed to support Operation VIGILANT WARRIOR.

(National Archives)

over the *Al Mahrousa* to the Kuwaitis for further investigation.[186] This incident was the first time anyone had apprehended a tanker violating UN sanctions against Iraq, which demonstrated the difficulty of enforcing the oil embargo not the rarity of Iraqi oil smuggling. The interdiction of the vessel also strengthened the U.S. and British argument against lifting the UN sanctions that Iraq had just violated.

Operation VIGILANT WARRIOR, which officially ended 22 December 1994, yielded several important outcomes. From a strategic perspective, the United States and its allies may have deterred Iraqi aggression with an agile and determined U.S.-led military force.[187] This was accomplished without firing a shot or sustaining a single casualty caused by enemy action. One military analyst called the operation "the first prominent example of effective conventional deterrence by the United States in the post–Cold War era."[188] Of course, this conclusion assumes that Saddam intended to attack Kuwait. U.S. Secretary of Defense William J. Perry believed as much.[189] Regardless, diplomatic efforts during the crisis led

---

186. Inal Ersan, "Tanker Captain Admits Loading Iraqi Diesel Oil," *Washington Post*, 25 Oct 1994.

187. Looking back a year later, President Clinton said, "I have stood in the desert of Kuwait with our vigilant warriors who stopped Iraqi aggression this time before it could start." William J. Clinton, *Public Papers of the Presidents of the United States: William J. Clinton, 1995, Book 1* (Washington, DC: Government Printing Office, 1996), 1733.

188. Herr, "Operation Vigilant Warrior," 8.

189. Speaking on 22 August 1995, Perry said, "There have been some unusual deployments of Iraqi military forces—nothing that leads us to believe that any invasion is underway or planned—in particular, *nothing like we saw in October of 1994 which we believed was clearly indicative an invasion was planned.*" (Emphasis added.) William J. Perry, *Public Statements of William J. Perry Secretary of Defense, 1995*, vol. 4 (Washington, DC: Historical Office,

to a UN-mandated ground exclusion zone, which curtailed the Iraqi military's freedom of movement and made deterrence easier in the future.

Other strategic victories proved a net gain for Kuwait and its allies against Iraq and its supporters. Saddam withdrew his threat to cease cooperating with UN inspectors and said he would comply fully with UN resolutions. Moreover, Iraq would now recognize the sovereignty of Kuwait, which it formerly claimed as Iraq's 19th Province, and acknowledge the new frontier, which ceded a corner of Umm Qasr and a disputed portion of the Rumaylah oil field to Kuwait. This gesture on Saddam's part cleared a major U.S. and British objection to the lifting of sanctions.

The Iraqi concession of recognizing the border was the product of intense behind-the-scenes Russian diplomacy. On 13 October, Russian foreign minister Andrei V. Kozyrev made a deal with Baghdad in which Iraq would agree to recognize Kuwait's sovereignty and the UN-designated border in exchange for renewed Russian efforts to end the sanctions within seven months.[190] Privately, Russian analysts believed Saddam had made an "unforgivable" mistake by provoking a confrontation just before the Security Council was to discuss Iraq's compliance with UNSCOM efforts.[191] This needless provocation assured that sanctions would remain in effect for the foreseeable future.

For the U.S. military, and the Army in particular, the rapid deployment of troops was the great achievement of the operation. General Gordon R. Sullivan, U.S. Army Chief of Staff, explained:

> The most recent crisis in Kuwait gave us the opportunity to demonstrate a new standard in rapid deployment. We alerted two Patriot batteries at Fort Polk, Louisiana, and they were in the air the next day. We alerted the 24th Infantry Division on a Friday; on Monday, planes began carrying the main body of the brigade to Kuwait. Within 10 days of the initial notification, the 1st Brigade Combat Team was in Kuwait and had drawn all of its pre-positioned equipment. Deploying a heavy brigade with this speed is a remarkable feat that we could not have accomplished five years ago—and which no other nation can do today.[192]

Although the Army put tens of thousands of soldiers on alert to deploy, the total number of U.S. soldiers in theater supporting Operation VIGILANT WARRIOR peaked at 6,987 on 27 October 1994.[193] This was a sizable force

Office of the Secretary of Defense, n.d.), 2676.

190. Judith Perera, "Russia's Measured Response," *Middle East International* (21 Oct 1994), 5.

191. Perera, "Russia's Measured Response," 6.

192. Gordon R. Sullivan, "A Vision for the Future," *Military Review* 75, no. 3 (May-Jun 1995): 6. The 1st Brigade Combat Team was a task-organized unit assembled around the 1st Brigade, 24th Infantry Division.

193. Gammons and Donnelly, *DAHSUM, FY 1995*, 47.

considering it had been transported across seven time zones in just four weeks with almost no warning.

From a joint perspective, the deployment was even more remarkable. Once assembled, U.S. forces in the Gulf included the CENTCOM forward headquarters, the ARCENT forward headquarters, two heavy brigade task forces, a Marine expeditionary unit, a carrier battle group, two Air Force squadrons, and significant support forces.[194] Total U.S. forces in theater reached their highest number of 28,952 on the last day of October.[195] General Peay boasted that "this impressive display of power projection achieved in days what had taken weeks during DESERT SHIELD."[196] This claim, while hyperbolic, pointed to the Army's improved ability to move its heavy units to the Middle East quickly. In 1990, it took the 24th Infantry Division seven weeks to move from Georgia to Saudi Arabia, with the first vessel carrying the division's equipment arriving a full two weeks after departing the United States.[197] In 1994, the first heavy companies were on the ground and moving to their dispersal areas in forty-eight hours, using the stockpile at Camp Doha. Even with the slowed pace of the deployment after Saddam backed down, the Army fielded two heavy brigade task forces in Kuwait in about a month. By contrast, the Marine Corps had needed roughly the same amount of time to deploy only one brigade—the 7th Marine Expeditionary Brigade—in 1990, using equipment and supplies that had been pre-positioned aboard ships in Diego Garcia.[198]

Despite the speed of the initial deployment, there was still room for improvement. It had worked out this time, but, privately, General Peay knew that things could have gone differently. In a meeting with General Shalikashvili on 16 October, Peay admitted that U.S. forces had faced

---

194. Williams, "Projection of Force," ch. 2, 17.
195. Puckett and Hines, "October Surprise," 76. In this document, "theater strength of U.S. forces" presumably includes all U.S. forces in the CENTCOM area of responsibility.
196. Quoted in Herr, "Operation Vigilant Warrior," 24.
197. One fast sealift ship carrying 24th Infantry Division equipment, USNS *Antares*, was towed to Rota, Spain, after breaking down in transit. The cargo was transferred to another vessel, which arrived in Saudi Arabia on 23 August 1990, three weeks behind the original schedule. Delays resulted from two out of five Maritime Pre-positioning Squadron 2 ships carrying 7th Marine Expeditionary Brigade's equipment being off station for maintenance. The MV *Fisher* was off the west coast of Africa en route to Blount Island in Jacksonville, Florida. The vessel turned around on 8 August and arrived at Al Jubayl, Saudi Arabia, on 14 August 1990. The MV *Baugh* was docked at Blount Island in Jacksonville, Florida, undergoing scheduled maintenance. The *Baugh* left port on 10 August and arrived at Al Jubayl on 5 September. James K. Matthews and Cora J. Holt, *So Many, So Much, So Far, So Fast: United States Transportation Command and Strategic Deployment for Operation Desert Shield / Desert Storm* (Washington, DC: Joint History Office, Chairman of the Joint Chiefs of Staff and the Research Center, U.S. Transportation Command, 1992), 119–23, 267–68, 292; Steven M. Zimmeck, *U.S. Marines in the Persian Gulf, 1990–1991 Combat Service Support in DESERT SHIELD and DESERT STORM* (Washington, DC: History and Museums Division Headquarters, U.S. Marine Corps, 1999), 7.
198. Matthews and Holt, *So Many, So Much*, 118, 267.

a window of vulnerability from 7 to 10 October. Had Saddam attacked during that period, the United States could have done little to stop him.

Critical gaps in the Army's planning and a shortage of equipment and supplies exacerbated the time-distance problem to which Peay alluded. Even though the Army had been training in Kuwait for three years, when the 24th Infantry Division arrived in theater it found no ground tactical plan for defending the emirate.[199] Even more disturbing was the absence or deficiency of many kinds of critical materiel in the war reserves, from multiple launch rocket systems (MLRSs) to engineering equipment to counterbattery radars to tactical maps to field sanitation kits. In an interview, General DeFrancisco also complained about "an almost tragic shortage of trucks."[200] The lack of equipment and supplies indicated that CENTCOM had not adequately prepared for a potential war in Kuwait, a problem that predated Peay's tenure. In fact, before advance parties arrived to inspect the stockpiles, soldiers drawing the equipment did not know what was on hand because no one could locate up-to-date inventories.[201] General Peay used the lessons he had learned during Operation VIGILANT WARRIOR to produce a new CENTCOM theater strategy and updated war plan for Iraq.[202]

In most cases, the soldiers on the ground had found workarounds to these sorts of problems, as assessed in the 24th Infantry Division's after action report. Because AWR-5 did not have sufficient engineering equipment, a single company of engineers supported two battalion task forces. A shortage of radios with encryption necessitated communicating tactical information in the clear—a cumbersome affair because of security precautions. S. Sgt. Grant R. Rosen of Company C, 3d Battalion, 69th Armor, explained how radio operators reported grid coordinates in code, using the words "camel turds" as the key in which each letter of the phrase stands for a number from 0 to 9.[203] Fortunately, the hastily assembled and minimally equipped force was not put to the test.

Some critics of Operation VIGILANT WARRIOR, including the French defense minister François G. M. Léotard, accused President Clinton of playing politics with the military ahead of the November 1994 midterm congressional elections.[204] However, no evidence suggests that Clinton's

---

199. AAR, Opn VIGILANT WARRIOR, HQ, 24th Inf Div, 19 Jan 1995, tab B, "Initial Impressions Report," 10, Operation VIGILANT WARRIOR Collection, CMH.
200. Interv, Maj. Michael W. Byrne with Maj. Gen. Joseph E. DeFrancisco, 9 Nov 1994, 32, CMH Catalog No. VWIT–A–010, Opn VIGILANT WARRIOR Collection, CMH.
201. Puckett and Hines, "October Surprise," 78. Compare to AAR, Opn VIGILANT WARRIOR, HQ, 24th Inf Div, 19 Jan 1995, tab B, "Initial Impressions Report," 5–6.
202. Strategic plan, U.S. Central Command, *Shaping U.S. Central Command for the 21st Century, 1995–1997,* n.d., 8, Historians Files, CMH.
203. Interv, Maj. Michael W. Byrne, with soldiers from Co C, 3d Bn, 69th Armor, 28 Nov 1994, CMH Catalog No. VWIT–A–0282b, Opn VIGILANT WARRIOR Collection, CMH.
204. William Drozdiak, "France Implies Domestic Politics in U.S. Sparked Response to Iraq," *Washington Post,* 13 Oct 1994, http://www.washingtonpost.com/archive/politics/1994/10/13/france-implies-domestic-politics-in-us-sparked-response-to-iraq/63549b58-1ba3-45ad-8ea8-6ed4d972dc2a/.

resolve in the face of Iraqi aggression was a ploy to gain more votes for members of his Democratic Party. Senate Minority Leader Robert J. "Bob" Dole, a Republican, supported the president's decision to send troops to the Middle East, even though Dole had opposed U.S. intervention in Haiti the month before. In any case, Republicans won the majority in both houses of Congress, flipping the leadership of both chambers.

Others, including some in the intelligence community, claimed that the United States had overreacted. It is true that early in the crisis, General Peay had told his staff that he "would rather take the heat for overreacting than be responsible for getting a lot of kids killed because we weren't prepared."[205] But assessing the validity of the charge that the United States had overreacted would require knowing what was in Saddam's mind, which no one did at the time. In 2003, after being captured by American soldiers, Saddam told his CIA interrogator that the 1994 troop movements were just exercises meant to keep the United States and Kuwait guessing about his intentions.[206] Although the threat was real at the time, the unexpected *Republican Guard* deployment may have been a misguided show of force intended to bully the UN Security Council into ending or easing sanctions and to distract from the deteriorating domestic situation they were causing.[207] Even though Saddam did not achieve sanctions relief and had to make concessions after withdrawing his troops from the border, he continued to test the resolve of the United States. But never again did Iraq use ground troops to threaten Kuwait.

After the confrontation with Iraq, the Third Army continued to improve its warfighting capabilities through numerous exercises. This headquarters participated in seven major exercises, including command post and field training varieties.[208] The cumulative effect of real-world deterrence operations, like Operation VIGILANT WARRIOR, and recurring scenario-driven exercises, such as INTRINSIC ACTION, improved ARCENT's ability and that of its subordinate commands to deploy to the Middle East and operate in harsh desert conditions. Less than a year after VIGILANT WARRIOR, another situation in Iraq would test these skills again as the Army rushed another heavy brigade to Kuwait to deter Saddam Hussein.

---

205. Peay, "XO's Notes," 11.
206. John Nixon, *Debriefing the President: The Interrogation of Saddam Hussein* (New York: Blue Rider Press, 2016), 113–14.
207. A recording of a 1994 conversation between the Iraqi president and his officials confirms this assessment. Kevin M. Woods, David D. Palkki, and Mark E. Stout, *The Saddam Tapes: The Inner Workings of a Tyrant's Regime, 1978–2001* (Cambridge, UK: Cambridge University Press, 2013), 265–67.
208. Annual Historical Review, Third U.S. Army, FY 1997, 6 Oct 1998, 1, Annual History Rpt Collection, CMH.

The discovery of Iraq's previously hidden biological weapons program led to another crisis in the fall of 1995. Earlier that year, UNSCOM inspectors found evidence of a more extensive operation than they previously imagined. The UNSCOM report to the UN Security Council in June, however, was mixed, declaring that "significant progress had been achieved" but stating that Iraq was still not accounting for its biological weapons material.[209] On 1 July 1995, Iraq admitted for the first time to the existence of an offensive biological weapons program but denied that it had attached biological agents to any weapons systems. Iraq tried unsuccessfully to paper over the disclosure, saying it would not be forthcoming about its biological weapons program until UNSCOM "closed the file" on its missile and chemical weapons programs.[210] When UNSCOM refused to certify Iraq's compliance and requested additional information, Saddam again threatened to end cooperation with the inspectors. Once more, Ekéus flew to Baghdad to negotiate an end to the impasse. Deputy Prime Minister Tariq Aziz repeated Saddam's threat to end cooperation unless UNSCOM certified Iraq's compliance with the sanctions regime.

The same day Ekéus reported Iraq's demands to the UN Security Council, an unexpected event dramatically changed the situation.[211] The regime was already on edge because of a rebellion and planned coup attempt by the Sunni Dulaimi tribe, a revolt which the central government had suppressed in June.[212] Then on 7 August, a crisis rocked the Iraqi leadership: Lt. Gen. Hussein Kamel, who had led part of Iraq's WMD program, fled to Jordan with his brother, Col. Saddam Kamel, the former head of the Iraqi presidential bodyguard.[213] Compounding the scandal, Hussein's wife Raghad and Saddam's wife Rana—both of whom were daughters of Saddam Hussein—left the country along with their husbands, who were also Saddam's second cousins. Internal politics

---

209. Cordesman, *Iraq and the War of Sanctions*, 212.

210. Clinton, *Public Papers of the Presidents of the United States: William J. Clinton, 1995, Book 1*, 1197.

211. Cordesman, *Iraq and the War of Sanctions*, 213.

212. Malovany, *Wars of Modern Babylon*, 648–49.

213. For a discussion of the various positions that Hussein Kamel held in the Iraqi government from 1987 until 1995, see Charles Duelfer, "Iraq's Military Industrial Capability—Evolution of the Military Industrialization Commission," in *Addendums to the Comprehensive Report of the Special Advisor to the DCI on Iraq's WMD* (Washington, DC: Central Intelligence Agency, Mar 2005), 5–7.

and family infighting were key factors in the Kamel brothers' defection. Saddam Hussein had recently given his eldest son, Uday, the position of Supervisor of the *Republican Guard,* displacing Hussein Kamel, whom Uday viewed as a rival and threat.[214] Kamel's flight to Jordan and subsequent revelations about Iraq's WMD programs demonstrated that Saddam's hold on power, propped up by nepotism and clan loyalty, rested on shaky foundations.[215] To Saddam, moreover, the defection of his sons-in-law was more than just a security breach; it was a personal betrayal.

The information Hussein Kamel brought to Jordan became a boon to UN inspectors and Western intelligence agencies. Before his defection, Kamel had hidden more than 600,000 pages of documents related to Iraq's WMD and missile programs, storing them in boxes on a chicken farm. These "chicken farm papers," which he took with him to Jordan, revealed secrets Iraq had hidden from UNSCOM and the IAEA. Of special interest were disclosures about the biological agents botulinum and anthrax being put on weapons, additional information about Iraq's nuclear weapons program, and evidence concerning Iraq's efforts to develop the highly toxic VX nerve agent.[216] The other WMD programs were already well known to the inspectors, who had made considerable progress in dismantling them. Apparently, Saddam wanted to maintain both the pretense of cooperation with inspectors as well as the ability to quickly restart these programs after the UN lifted sanctions. The new revelations about Iraq's WMD programs delayed this goal.

Not only did Kamel hand over damaging evidence of Iraq's noncompliance with UN inspectors, but also he claimed (albeit without evidence) that Saddam had been planning to invade Kuwait and Saudi Arabia and had called off the attack when Kamel fled.[217] At the time of Kamel's departure, the Iraqi military was continuing five weeks of unusual troop movements in and around their garrisons, at surface-to-air missile sites, and at air bases.[218] Combined with the high-level defection and claims of a recently aborted invasion of Kuwait, the Iraqi training exercises caused alarm in Washington, even though the United States did not detect evidence that Saddam was moving troops to the Kuwaiti border. In fact, Secretary of Defense William J. Perry had observed that

---

214. Malovany, *Wars of Modern Babylon,* 644; Amatzia Baram, "Building Toward Crisis: Saddam Husayn's Strategy for Survival," Policy Paper no. 47 (Washington, DC: Washington Institute for Near East Policy, 1998), 10–13.

215. Marr, *Modern History of Iraq,* 241.

216. Although the documents revealed previously hidden material about the extent of Iraq's weapons of mass destruction programs, secondary literature on the topic does not indicate that the biological weapons program continued after the Persian Gulf War. For example, see Cordesman, *Iraq and the War of Sanctions,* 213–15; Malovany, *Wars of Modern Babylon,* 616–18.

217. Associated Press, "Defector Says Iraq Planned Invasion," *Washington Post,* 21 Aug 1995.

218. Herbert C. Banks, ed., *1st Cavalry Division: A Spur Ride through the 20th Century, "From Horses to the Digital Battlefield"* (Paducah, KY: Turner, 2002), 133.

there was "nothing that leads us to believe that any invasion is underway or planned."[219] Still, the Clinton administration was concerned that Saddam might behave aggressively as he had the previous October.[220]

As a precaution, the United States rushed 1,500 Army troops to the Persian Gulf, moving up the next INTRINSIC ACTION exercise that had been scheduled for October. Within forty-eight hours of being alerted, elements of Col. John S. Brown's 2d Brigade, 1st Cavalry Division, made the 8,000-mile flight from Fort Hood, Texas, to Kuwait. The main body was Task Force 1–5, formed around elements of 1st Battalion, 5th Cavalry, and composed of two tank companies and two mechanized infantry companies plus support units. To augment this task force, the joint staff authorized an additional tank company, an artillery battalion with an MLRS battery, an engineering company, and enough support elements for an entire brigade.[221] The trigger for deploying the rest of the brigade would be an unambiguous Iraqi threat in the form of combat units moving toward the border. The joint chiefs also ordered thirteen pre-positioned ships, including those carrying AWR-3, to head toward the Persian Gulf.[222] One aircraft carrier, USS *Abraham Lincoln*, which was due to depart the Gulf, remained until the USS *Independence* could arrive as its relief. Another carrier, USS *Theodore Roosevelt*, proceeded to the eastern Mediterranean to enhance a combined U.S.-Jordanian military exercise, INFINITE MOONLIGHT, already underway in the desert south of Amman.[223] This exercise, involving 2,000 U.S. Marines, served as a convenient deterrence force during the heightened state of readiness.[224] As in Operation VIGILANT WARRIOR, the Third Army deployed General Taylor to Kuwait to head ARCENT (Forward), providing command and control of ground operations during what now was Operation VIGILANT SENTINEL. This theater army headquarters element, excessive for the size of the task force in Kuwait at the time, served as a precaution in case additional units deployed.

The task force's mission was to deter a possible Iraqi attack on Kuwait and Saudi Arabia through a show of force. When this threat did not materialize, the operation turned into an expanded INTRINSIC ACTION exercise. The first companies to arrive in Kuwait drew their vehicles and heavy equipment from AWR-5 and moved out in record time, averaging less than six hours. Colonel Brown reported that "once on the ground

---

219. Perry, *Public Statements of William J. Perry Secretary of Defense, 1995*, vol. 4, 2676.
220. Clinton, *Public Papers of the Presidents of the United States: William J. Clinton, 1995, Book 1*, 1673.
221. Brown, *Kevlar Legions*, 104; Dee Constant, "Mission Accomplished: After a Successful Coalition CALFEX, Task Force 1-5 Prepares to Leave," *Desert Voice* 8, no. 7 (16 Oct 1995): 1.
222. Clinton, *Public Papers of the Presidents of the United States: William J. Clinton, 1995, Book 1*, 1673. Compare to Brown, *Kevlar Legions*, 105.
223. INFINITE MOONLIGHT was a bilateral U.S.-Jordanian military exercise, which Jordan hosted annually during the 1990s and beyond.
224. Brown, *Kevlar Legions*, 104.

they conducted reconnaissance and maneuvered their units through the ground they were to defend, refining the contingency plan into an operational plan."[225] On the Udari Range complex, Task Force 1–5 conducted separate live-fire exercises with a battalion landing team of U.S. Marines and with the Kuwaiti 6th Mechanized Brigade. The culmination of the U.S.-Kuwaiti training was a large-scale combined-arms, live-fire exercise through swaths of open desert. Three months into their mission, the 2d Brigade, 1st Cavalry Division, conducted a relief-in-place with the 3d Brigade, 4th Infantry Division, from Fort Carson, Colorado.[226] Through repeated exercises in Kuwait, coalition forces honed their ability to respond to actual contingencies.

Meanwhile, the Iraqi military had been preparing for a future conflict with a U.S.-led coalition. In April 1995, a reorganization transformed the *Republican Guard* into an independent army, parallel to the regular army and having its own general staff and two corps headquarters. That same month, Saddam replaced his air force commander, Lt. Gen. Muzahim Sa'ab Hassan, with Hassan's deputy, Maj. Gen. Khaldun Khattab Bakr. Saddam had already replaced the army aviation commander the previous year. These personnel shifts were part of a broader Iraqi effort to defeat coalition aircraft patrolling the no-fly zones, an activity which Saddam saw as an illegal encroachment on his nation's sovereignty because the patrols lacked UN authorization. Saddam had even brought in advisers—from Vietnam in 1995 and 1999 and from Yugoslavia in 2000—to help develop a strategy to defeat coalition aircraft.[227] The Iraqi air defense command developed ways of neutralizing HARMs (high-speed, antiradiation missiles).[228] At the time of the Kamel defection in early September, the Iraqi military was conducting training across all of its service branches. Thus, while UN sanctions constrained Iraq's ability to rearm and modernize its military, the nation was far from dormant in preparing for war.

The papers that Hussein Kamel smuggled out of Iraq highlighted Saddam's obfuscation and further eroded the regime's credibility. Although the UN had ample evidence for Iraqi noncompliance even before Kamel's defection, the new revelations were staggering. They showed that Saddam had lied about his biological weapons just a few months prior, and that he continued to pursue nuclear weapons even after the end of the Gulf War. When Kamel left Iraq, Saddam, apparently fearful of what his son-in-law would reveal, quickly invited UN inspectors to examine previously undisclosed information about his weapons program. He also offered the implausible explanation that Kamel had hidden all this information from both the inspectors and Saddam himself.[229]

225. Brown, *Kevlar Legions*, 105.
226. Brown, *Kevlar Legions*, 105–6.
227. Woods, *Iraqi Perspectives Report*, 34n28.
228. Malovany, *Wars of Modern Babylon*, 630.
229. Clinton, *Public Papers of the Presidents of the United States: William J. Clinton, 1995, Book 1*, 1672.

A chilling postscript to the story of the Kamel brothers' defection epitomizes both Saddam Hussein's brutality and the tribal nature of Iraqi society. In February 1996, the Iraqi president lured his sons-in-law back to Iraq with a public pardon. Saddam then had them, but not his daughters, killed along with other members of the extended Kamel family. Saddam carefully selected the assassins from among his own relatives to illustrate that this was a family matter and not an act of state. This revenge killing shows how personally and violently Saddam reacted to disloyalty. Later that year, four or five men shot and nearly killed Saddam's son Uday while he was driving down a west Baghdad street. Uday's wounds were severe enough to require multiple surgeries and render him no longer viable as a candidate to succeed his father. At least six opposition groups claimed responsibility for the attack.[230] One theory held that a Shi'a opposition group from the marshes of southern Iraq was responsible.[231] Another theory claimed the attack was carried out by relatives of the Kamel brothers as revenge for their deaths.[232]

Even after the Kamel episode, Iraq continued its mixed record of compliance with UN inspections. On 10 November 1995, Jordan intercepted a shipment of Russian-made missile guidance systems bound for Iraq.[233] Throughout most of 1996, Iraq denied UNSCOM access to several facilities the commission wanted to inspect and refused a records request related to Scud missiles still in the Iraqi arsenal. Nevertheless, UNSCOM made some progress. In May, Iraq finally agreed to an oil-for-food program, approved by the UN for a second time the previous year, which allowed Iraq, under UN supervision, to sell $2 billion worth of oil for food and medical supplies. This move came after inflation drove down the buying power of the Iraqi dinar to its lowest point yet.[234] In June, UNSCOM dismantled the Al Hakum facility, which had been Iraq's largest and most sophisticated biological weapons plant. That same month, Ekéus visited Baghdad to discuss Iraqi objections to inspections at what they called "sensitive sites."[235] What followed was a familiar pattern of limited progress and heavy resistance to the inspections regime.

While keeping a watchful eye on Iraq, the U.S. Army conducted more than just deterrence operations. In 1995, the United States continued and expanded its biannual training exercise in the Egyptian desert. Operation BRIGHT STAR, a multinational, live-fire field training exercise, had grown out of the 1978 Camp David Accords and had occurred in Egypt every two years since 1980. These exercises strengthened ties between the U.S. and Egyptian militaries and demonstrated the American ability to rapidly reinforce its allies in the Middle East. The robust training

---

230. Baram, "Building Toward Crisis," 18.
231. Marr, *Modern History of Iraq*, 242.
232. Baram, "Building Toward Crisis," 18.
233. Cordesman, *Iraq and the War of Sanctions*, 216.
234. Marr, *Modern History of Iraq*, 239.
235. Malovany, *Wars of Modern Babylon*, 617.

General Taylor and Colonel Brown during Operation VIGILANT SENTINEL
(Desert Voice)

Americans conducted with their Egyptian counterparts involved "ground maneuver, live fire, airborne, air assault and the entire range of combat support and service support operations."[236] The BRIGHT STAR 95 exercise included nearly 60,000 troops, both active duty and reserve, from the United States, Egypt, the United Arab Emirates, France, and the United Kingdom. Coalition building remained an important part of the U.S. strategic approach in the Middle East.

The Army conducted large-scale operations outside the Middle East as well. In the mid-1990s, U.S. military involvement in the Balkans deepened. At the end of the Cold War, the break-up of ethnically and religiously diverse Yugoslavia had caused the UN to assume a peacekeeping role. The UN Protection Force assembled for this task became "the largest and most expensive UN peacekeeping operation in history."[237] Bosnian Serbs, backed by nationalist Serbia, revolted when Bosnia and Herzegovina formed as a new nation with a Bosnian Muslim plurality and a smaller Christian Serbian minority, who wanted their own independent Serb republic.[238] In 1992, after civil war broke out in Bosnia, the Serbian military laid siege to Sarajevo, the Bosnian capital, and, with the help of Bosnian Serbs, pursued a brutal campaign of village-by-village

---

236. James R. Ellis, "Third . . . Always First!" *ARMY Magazine* 44, no. 10 (Oct 1994): 119.
237. Stewart, *American Military History*, vol. 2, 444.
238. After the breakup of the Socialist Federal Republic of Yugoslavia (1945–1992), Serbia remained one of two constituent states, along with Montenegro, that made up the successor state, the Federal Republic of Yugoslavia (1992–2003). The Serb republic, called Republika Srpska, attempted unsuccessfully to win full independence during the 1992–1994 Bosnian War and became one of two political entities within Bosnia and Herzegovina after the 1995 U.S.-brokered Dayton Agreement. The other political entity within the new nation was the Federation of Bosnia and Herzegovina with mostly Bosniak and Croat residents.

Soldiers from the 96th Transportation Company, 180th Transportation Battalion, load an M113 armored personnel carrier onto a commercial heavy equipment transporter during Operation VIGILANT SENTINEL, 1995.
(Desert Voice)

ethnic cleansing. In 1995, NATO and the United States increased their involvement to stop the violence. The U.S.-brokered peace agreement in the fall of 1995 led to a larger peacekeeping role for NATO and the United States. NATO launched Operation JOINT ENDEAVOR.[239] The multinational Implementation Force for this mission grew to 60,000 troops including 20,000 U.S. personnel.[240] During the 1990s, troop-heavy deployments—to Somalia, Haiti, Bosnia, and later, Kosovo—occupied more of the Army's attention and resources. Except during brief times of looming crisis, deterrence operations against Iraq were a secondary concern.

239. "History of the NATO-led Stabilisation Force (SFOR) in Bosnia and Herzegovina," SFOR Stabilisation Force, https://www.nato.int/sfor/docu/d981116a.htm.
240. Stewart, *American Military History*, vol. 2, 446. The Implementation Force became the Stabilization Force a year later, and Operation JOINT ENDEAVOR transitioned into Operation JOINT GUARD.

On 13 November 1995, a car bomb exploded outside a U.S. training facility in Riyadh, Saudi Arabia, killing seven people, including five Americans, and injuring about sixty others.[241] The explosion ripped the facade off the Office of the Program Manager–Saudi Arabian National Guard headquarters building, occupied by approximately 400 American military personnel who trained Saudi guardsmen to use weapons bought from the United States. This attack, which garnered little public attention at the time, revealed increasing opposition to the ongoing U.S. military presence in the Kingdom of Saudi Arabia, at least among radical Muslims. It also foreshadowed the growing threat of terrorism in the region.

After the attack in Riyadh, American military personnel in Saudi Arabia remained vulnerable. Terrorists struck again in an even more devastating way on 25 June 1996 when a suicide bomber driving an explosive-laden truck attacked the Khobar Towers, a barracks complex in Dhahran, which housed U.S. Air Force personnel supporting Operation SOUTHERN WATCH. This attack killed nineteen Americans and one Saudi and wounded nearly 500 people.

Although Iran denied responsibility for this terrorist attack, the evidence eventually pointed to Shi'a Saudi nationals with links to Hezbollah, the pro-Iranian group in Lebanon. David B. Crist, a historian at the Pentagon, claimed, "American communications intercepts confirmed the knowledge [of the attack] at the highest levels of the Iranian government and the approval of the supreme leader."[242] If the United States determined that Iran was behind the attack, as Crist has suggested, then U.S. government leaders must have decided it best not to publicize the fact. Because a direct attack on a U.S. military base constitutes an act of war, publicly accusing the Iranians of approving the bombing would have backed the United States into a corner where anything shy of a military response would seem too weak. Silence allowed for other, covert options.[243]

---

241. Jamie McIntyre, "U.S. Vows Terrorist Bomb Won't Affect Saudi Relationship," CNN World News, 13 Nov 1995, http://www.cnn.com/WORLD/9511/saudi_blast/pm/. Compare to Perry D. Jameson, *Khobar Towers: Tragedy and Response* (Washington, DC: Air Force History and Museums Program, 2008), 23.
242. Crist, *Twilight War*, 405. See also Jameson, *Khobar Towers*, 195–98.
243. Crist, *Twilight War*, 409. See also Richard A. Clarke, *Against All Enemies: Inside America's War on Terror* (New York: Free Press, 2004), 111–21.

Memorial display at the headquarters of the Office of Program Manager–Saudi Arabian National Guard, commemorating the twenty-fifth anniversary of the 13 November 1995 terrorist bombing in Riyadh

Nevertheless, when American military personnel die tragically, an investigation inevitably follows. Three days after the Khobar Towers bombing, Defense Secretary Perry appointed General Wayne A. Downing, former Commander in Chief, U.S. Special Operations Command, to conduct an assessment of the facts and circumstances surrounding the bombing. Although the Downing Report pointed to multiple failures throughout the chain of command, it assigned the largest share of blame to Air Force Brig. Gen. Terryl J. Schwalier, commander of the 4404th Composite Wing, because he "did not adequately protect his forces from a terrorist attack."[244] The commission's report bothered Marine Corps Lt. Gen. Anthony C. Zinni, who had replaced Neal as CENTCOM's deputy commander in chief. Among other recommendations, the report called for a host of physical security measures, including cable-linked

---

244. DoD, Gen. Wayne A. Downing et al., *Report to the President and Congress on the Protection of U.S. Forces Deployed Abroad*, Rpt to Cong., 30 Aug 1996, finding 20, 50, https://fas.org/irp/threat/downing/unclf913.html. See also Jameson, *Khobar Towers*, 187.

Jersey barriers, and expensive electronic surveillance technologies to detect intruders. Zinni later explained, "We have been stalked by terrorists. And they're still after us. Yet in order to do our mission, we have to take risks."[245] In addition, overseas bases require the approval of the host nation in order to make improvements to infrastructure and perimeter security, and foreign officials often are reluctant to permit fortress-like structures, especially for a mission such as SOUTHERN WATCH, which was supposed to be temporary.

While General Downing investigated the bombing, Secretary Perry focused on improving force protection measures. In July, he announced that "as many as 4,000 American military personnel stationed in Riyadh, Dhahran, and perhaps other Saudi cities would move into more remote sites in the desert."[246] As airmen from the Khobar Towers complex relocated to Prince Sultan Air Base, more than 100 kilometers southeast of Riyadh, a new crisis arose in Iraq.

Immediately after the Khobar Towers attack, U.S. intelligence efforts in Iraq suffered a serious setback. On 26 June, the day after the bombing in Saudi Arabia, Saddam began arresting at least 200 of his military officers in and around Baghdad. He executed eighty of them. This brutal reprisal came in the wake of a failed coup d'état. The CIA had coordinated with Ayad Allawi, an exiled Iraqi Shi'a who was the head of the Iraqi National Accord, to form an opposition group committed to the ouster of Saddam Hussein and the overthrow of his Baathist regime.[247] Working inside the protected Kurdish zone in northern Iraq, the CIA had gathered intelligence, broadcast propaganda, and trained Iraqi military defectors in the hopes that they would topple Iraq's government. Despite two years of planning and millions of dollars invested in the effort, Saddam's spies infiltrated the network and foiled the plot.[248]

A conflict between two Kurdish militias gave Saddam's government an advantage over U.S.-backed dissident groups. The forces of the Patriotic Union of Kurdistan (PUK) routed those of the Kurdistan Democratic

---

245. Tom Clancy with Gen. (Ret.) Tony Zinni and Tony Koltz, *Battle Ready* (New York: Putnam, 2004), 305.
246. Jameson, *Khobar Towers*, 181. Compare to Philip Shenon, "For Safety, Pentagon May Scatter G.I.'s Around Saudi Arabia," *New York Times*, 18 Jul 1996.
247. According to a report for Congress, "One group, the Iraqi National Accord (INA), consisted primarily of military and security officers who had defected from Iraq and who were perceived to have some residual influence in Baghdad. The INA had received U.S. and Saudi backing in 1991 and 1992, before the INC [Iraqi National Congress] came into favor in Washington." Kenneth Katzman, *Iraq's Opposition Movements*, 98–179F (Washington, DC: Congressional Research Service, 4 Sep 1998, updated 27 Jun 2000), 3. See also Ali A. Allawi, *The Occupation of Iraq: Winning the War, Losing the Peace* (New Haven, CT: Yale University Press, 2007), 67–68. For a CIA field officer's first-hand account of a failed effort to overthrow the Iraqi regime the previous year, see Robert Baer, *See No Evil: The True Story of a Ground Soldier in the CIA's War on Terrorism* (New York: Crown, 2002), 177–213.
248. Tim Weiner, *Legacy of Ashes: The History of the CIA* (New York: Anchor, 2007), 534–35; Tim Weiner, "For 3d Time in 21 Years, Saddam Hussein's Foes Pay Price for Foiled U.S. Plot," *New York Times*, 11 Sep 1996.

Khobar Towers after a terrorist bombing in Dhahran, Saudi Arabia, on 25 June 1996
(*Department of Defense*)

Party (KDP), prompting the KDP, which had opposed Saddam Hussein in the past, to ask his government for help. Ignoring strong U.S. warnings, the Iraqi president ordered approximately 30,000 troops into the Kurds' enclave in northern Iraq.[249] On 31 August 1996, the Iraqi army and KDP forces overran Erbil, the provisional Kurdish capital, forcing the PUK defenders to flee into the mountains. On their approach to the city, Iraqi forces captured and executed ninety-six members of Ahmed Chalabi's pro-Western Iraqi National Congress, an umbrella opposition group fighting alongside the PUK.[250] Iraq's aggression once again shocked the international community and caused hurried evacuations of both the Iraqi National Congress headquarters and a covert CIA station.[251] While campaigning in Tennessee ahead of the upcoming presidential elections, Clinton expressed his grave concern about the situation in Iraq and indicated that he had put the U.S. military on high alert. The response, which military planners were in the process of drawing up, would become Operation DESERT STRIKE.

On 3 September, Clinton ordered retaliatory measures against Iraq "to make Saddam pay a price for the latest act of brutality [against the

---

249. For the number of Iraqi troops, see Jonathan C. Randal, "Fleeing Iraqi Kurds Turned back by Iran," *Washington Post*, 11 Sep 1996. After deleting one division in 1995 and another in 1996, the Iraqi army consisted of twenty-three divisions, including seventeen regular army and six *Republican Guard*. Malovany, *Wars of Modern Babylon*, 606.
250. Knights, *Cradle of Conflict*, 155–56. Iraqi National Congress Executive Director Ahmed Chalabi, a secular Shi'a Muslim and U.S.-trained mathematician, had fled Iraq for Jordan in the late 1950s and eventually chaired the Petra Bank there. Katzman, *Iraq's Opposition Movements*, 2.
251. Weiner, "For 3d Time in 21 Years, Saddam Hussein's Foes Pay Price for Foiled U.S. Plot."

civilian population of Erbil], reducing his ability to threaten his neighbors and America's interests."[252] CENTCOM had planned airstrikes—not in the north where Iraqi aggression was taking place but in the south, because it was neither politically nor militarily feasible to attack the Iraqi army in the north. U.S. leaders decided not to ask Turkey for permission to launch airstrikes from their country to aid the PUK, because this group cooperated with the Kurdish Workers Party, which was in armed rebellion against the government in Ankara. The United States asked Saudi Arabia to allow strikes from their country instead, which implied the United States was planning attacks in southern Iraq. However, King Fahd refused to allow the use of Saudi air bases to attack Iraq.[253] The Saudi monarch was concerned about the reaction of Islamic extremists in the wake of the two anti-American terrorist attacks in his kingdom, and he also viewed Saddam's conflict with the Kurds as an internal matter— one that did not pose a threat to Iraq's neighbors.

Without the use of Saudi air bases, the United States employed cruise missiles to attack fourteen air defense sites in southern Iraq— surface-to-air missile, radar, and command and control facilities—which could be used to target coalition aircraft patrolling the no-fly zones. On 3–4 September, the Navy launched thirty-one Tomahawks from two surface ships and one submarine in the Persian Gulf while the Air Force fired thirteen cruise missiles from B–52s.[254] Among the allies, only the British supported these attacks, though their participation was limited to allowing the U.S. Air Force to use the base in Diego Garcia.[255] President Clinton also announced an extension of the southern no-fly zone 60 nautical miles northward to the 33rd parallel, near the southern suburbs of Baghdad.[256] (See Map 5, page 36.) After the destruction of the Iraqi air defenses, coalition aircraft could operate more freely in the extended exclusion zone. As with his predecessor's decision to create the no-fly zones without UN approval, Clinton made the boundary change unilaterally, leading France to declare that its pilots would not patrol above the 32nd parallel. As a result of the extension, Iraq shifted some aircraft farther north, despite Saddam's claim that he would no longer honor the two no-fly zones. In addition to the unilateral U.S. measures, UN Secretary General Boutros Boutros-Ghali announced a delay in the implementation of the oil-for-food program because of the deteriorating situation in Iraq.[257] This postponement became necessary because Erbil was a key distribution

---

252. Clinton, *Public Papers of the Presidents of the United States: William J. Clinton, 1996, Book 2*, 1469.

253. Jameson, *Khobar Towers*, 184.

254. Perry, *Public Statements of William J. Perry Secretary of Defense, 1996–97*, vol. 3, 1531.

255. Perry, *Public Statements of William J. Perry Secretary of Defense, 1996–97*, vol. 3, 1531, 1534.

256. Perry, *Public Statements of William J. Perry Secretary of Defense, 1996–97*, vol. 3, 1530.

257. David Dahl, "U.S. Weighing Response to Iraqi Invasion," *St. Petersburg Times*, 2 Sep 1996.

center for the aid purchased through this program, and the UN wanted to make sure that humanitarian supplies would get to all who needed them.

Under pressure, Saddam began backing down after his blitz attack on the north. By 4 September, the Iraqi heavy forces had withdrawn from Erbil and appeared to be returning to their garrisons.[258] Even as the Iraqi troops continued to redeploy, on 9 September the KDP consolidated its gains by taking As Sulaymaniyah, an important cultural center, without firing a shot. The bulk of the Iraqi forces were out of the north within a few days, and the rest were gone by 14 September.[259] In order to stop another Kurdish refugee crisis like that of 1991, Saddam declared a general amnesty, echoed by KDP leader Masoud Barzani, encouraging fleeing Kurds—estimated by the UN to number between 50,000 and 75,000—to return home.[260] Iran closed its border to Kurdish refugees, giving them little choice but to turn back.

Saddam's withdrawal of Iraqi ground troops from the north did not mean that he was willing to let the extension of the southern no-fly zone go unchallenged. On 11 September, Iraq fired three surface-to-air missiles at coalition aircraft, but all three missed their intended targets. On 13 September, while the 4404th Composite Wing was in the middle of its move to Prince Sultan Air Base, the Iraqis fired SA–6 surface-to-air missiles at three F–16 fighters patrolling the no-fly zone. Again, all missed their targets. This Iraqi aggression, combined with the Saudis' refusal to allow their bases to be used for offensive operations, caused the Air Force to send a squadron and a half of the Saudi-based F–16s to Shaikh Isa Air Base in Bahrain. The move freed these aircraft for missions other than patrolling. Kuwait permitted the basing of American F–117A Nighthawk stealth fighters on its soil, increasing the coalition's offensive capabilities in the region, and Clinton ordered a second aircraft carrier, USS *Enterprise*, to join the USS *Carl Vinson*, which was already in the Persian Gulf.

In addition to amplifying its Navy and Air Force presence, the United States increased its number of ground troops in the region. The 1st Battalion, 9th Cavalry, 1st Cavalry Division, was already in Kuwait for INTRINSIC ACTION 96–3, having arrived in early August.[261] Organized as Task Force 1–9, the unit comprised two tank and two mechanized companies, an artillery battery, an engineering company, and most of a forward support battalion. As a precaution against Iraqi aggression in the south, the United States sent approximately 3,500 soldiers to Kuwait in addition to the 1,200 or so already there. After Perry obtained permission from the Kuwaiti emir, the rest of Col. Eric

---

258. Clinton, *Public Papers of the Presidents of the United States: William J. Clinton, 1996, Book 2*, 1476; Knights, *Cradle of Conflict*, 166.
259. Knights, *Cradle of Conflict*, 167.
260. Randal, "Fleeing Iraqi Kurds Turned Back by Iran." Compare to Associated Press, "Iraq's Hussein Reasserts Control of Kurdish Area as Refugees Flee," *Tampa Tribune*, 11 Sep 1996.
261. Organized as an infantry battalion at the time, 1st Battalion, 9th Cavalry, was therefore designated as a battalion rather than a squadron.

T. Olson's 3d Brigade, 1st Cavalry Division, flew from Fort Hood to join their battalion already in the Gulf. Lead elements departed on 19 September, two days after notification, and began drawing equipment from pre-positioned stocks six hours after landing in Kuwait. By 21 September, the entire brigade had left Texas.[262] The president intended this deployment to demonstrate the United States' resolve to protect its allies and vital national interests in the region.

Task organized as the 3d Brigade Combat Team, the unit's mission was to deploy to theater, draw pre-positioned equipment and supplies, move into position, and prepare to defend the northern border of Kuwait in support of Operation DESERT STRIKE. Olson later wrote, "We took this mission as operational in nature, that is, we did *not* consider it to be a training mission at the time the deployment order was received. The BCT [brigade combat team] deployed to Kuwait ready to fight."[263] However, with no enemy forces attacking Kuwait, the deployment took on the familiar rhythms of a typical INTRINSIC ACTION exercise, albeit on a larger scale. Most of the newly arriving units completed their equipment draw and convoyed to the Udari Range within forty-eight hours of the lead elements' arrival. Ambassador Crocker said, "Seeing them come out, fly 20 hours, fall in on their equipment and deploy to the desert in another 6 to 8 hours makes me extremely proud to be an American."[264] This impressive timeline proved that a U.S.-based heavy brigade could function as a rapid deployment force for the Middle East.[265]

Conditions in the training area were harsh and the detritus of war provided a visual reminder of the Iraqi threat. Daytime temperatures soared above 120°F. First Lieutenant George H. Roberts III recalled, "On the way [to the Udari Range] we passed a vehicle graveyard of Iraqi tanks, trucks and assorted vehicles that were destroyed during the Gulf War. We couldn't stop at the time, although I had a chance later to go look at the vehicles. Some of the vehicles had personal items from Iraqi soldiers in them." Roberts later recalled an incident involving a snake that occurred while setting up a pistol range: "At one point soldiers left their rifles and began running from the range. A cobra had stood its head up and flattened it from behind some sandbags, hissing at the soldier[s]. A scout platoon staff sergeant took his 9mm and shot the snake, using 9 rounds before he hit it."[266] Hitting a venomous snake poised to strike proved more difficult than aiming at a silhouette paper target. While the infantrymen adjusted to a new environment, engineers made improvements to the assembly areas where the soldiers lived. They built floors for the tents and latrines with 55-gallon

---

262. Eric T. Olson, "3D Brigade (Grey Wolf), 1st Cavalry Division in Desert Strike," (Unpublished Rpt, n.d.), 3, Historians Files, CMH.
263. Olson, "3D Brigade (Grey Wolf)," 2–3. (Emphasis in the original.)
264. Olson, "3D Brigade (Grey Wolf)," 5.
265. Pre-positioned equipment and supplies in Kuwait made rapid deployment of a heavy brigade possible. The timeline would have been much longer in areas without a stockpile.
266. Memoir, Lt. Col. (Ret.) George H. Roberts III, "Memories," n.d., Historians Files, CMH.

metal drums under them. Every day a few soldiers had the unenviable task of burning the human waste.

Once on the ranges, the brigade combat team conducted live-fire and maneuver training on every level. Elements engaged in joint training with close air support provided by Air Force and Navy fighters. Bradley and tank crews performed gunnery exercises with increasing complexity. Iraqi vehicles abandoned during the Gulf War served as targets for live-fire drills, giving the exercise a realistic feel. The 2d Battalion, 82d Field Artillery, shot the newest version of self-propelled Paladin howitzers, becoming the first unit to test fire this weapon in Kuwait. Headquarters units also practiced their skills. JTF-Kuwait, under the command of the Third Army deputy, Maj. Gen. Robert R. Ivany, led command post exercises and planning activities with the various headquarters units. The different training events culminated with American, British, and Kuwaiti troops participating in a coalition combined-arms, live-fire exercise on 20 November. The Camp Doha *Desert Voice* newspaper described the scene:

> Kuwaiti FA–18 jets headed the assault against the notional enemy by dropping bombs against the attacking notional force. Then Kuwaiti and American tankers and artillerymen showered the targets, actual Iraqi vehicles destroyed in the Gulf War and now used as realistic training aids. British infantrymen, in fortified bunkers, fired on pop-up targets that simulated attacking dismounted troops.[267]

The USS *Laboon* fires a Tomahawk missile at Iraq in September 1996.
(U.S. Navy)

---

267. Dee Constant, "Task Force Successfully Deters Iraq," *Desert Voice* 9, no. 14 (1 Dec 1996): 15.

General Peay and Colonel Olson with troops in Kuwait during Operation DESERT STRIKE
(Desert Voice)

The Kuwaiti Armed Forces chief of staff, Lt. Gen. Ali al-Moumen said, "I hope he [Saddam Hussein] gets the message that we have a deterrent here, which he needs to take into consideration."[268] Despite fears of another Iraqi move on Kuwait in late 1996, none materialized. American units in Kuwait for DESERT STRIKE began to return to the United States during the first week of December with the last troops departing on 12 December.

Operation DESERT STRIKE illustrated the challenges of responding to Saddam's aggression against his own people. Saddam's military adventurism in the Kurdish enclave exposed two failures of U.S. foreign policy: the United States was unable to broker a peace deal among the competing Kurdish factions, and it could not fulfill its self-appointed role as the protector of the Iraqi Kurds. Saddam proved that the Kurdish "safe haven" in the north was not safe from Iraqi military intervention, even under the protective cover of a coalition no-fly zone. Multiple factors constrained the U.S. response, including the absence of U.S. ground troops in the north. Reliance upon neighboring states for basing and overflight rights also limited U.S. military options. Moreover, the president was caught between coalition partners, who urged restraint, and the Republican presidential nominee Senator Dole and his supporters, who accused Clinton of being soft on Iraq just weeks before the election. Clinton's response—in the form of limited cruise missile strikes in the south—represented what was both reasonable and possible under the circumstances. Combined with the extension of the southern no-fly zone (which lasted until the 2003 Iraq War) and an enlarged deterrence force in Kuwait, this approach sent the message to Saddam that he would pay a price for aggression, even within Iraq's borders.

---

268. Constant, "Task Force Successfully Deters Iraq," 15.

OPERATION
DESERT THUNDER

After Operation DESERT STRIKE, Iraq interfered with UN weapons inspectors with increasing frequency and temerity. By chipping away at the inspections regime, Saddam attempted to exploit the gap between nations that supported continuing sanctions, especially Great Britain and the United States, and those that were experiencing sanctions fatigue and wanted to normalize relations with Iraq, such as Russia, France, and China.

In June 1997, Iraqi escorts hindered the pilots of UNSCOM aircraft on four separate occasions. They "attempted to seize the controls of UN helicopters, deliberately flew too close to UNSCOM helicopters, and threatened to shut off the helicopter's fuel pumps in another incident."[269] This behavior drew a sharp rebuke from the UN Security Council.[270] Ekéus reported that Iraq blocked inspectors at three locations, having them wait for hours while Iraqis cleaned out the facilities and removed documents. On 6 October, Richard W. Butler, who had replaced Ekéus as the head of UNSCOM, submitted to the Security Council a report critical of Iraq, cataloging numerous violations as well as discrepancies in the latest Iraqi "full and final disclosure" report. As a result, the United States and Great Britain called for new sanctions to restrict Iraqi officials and intelligences officers from traveling overseas.[271]

Even as this crisis developed in Iraq, CENTCOM went ahead with its scheduled BRIGHT STAR 98 exercise, which ran from 12 October to 13 November 1997 in Egypt.[272] A deadly terrorist attack on German tourists in Cairo caused the United States to put the pyramids off limits to U.S. military personnel and provided a somber reminder of the importance of overseas force protection.[273] It also illustrated the complexities of the area of operations with its competing priorities.[274]

---

269. Cordesman, *Iraq and the War of Sanctions*, 219.

270. Graham S. Pearson, *The Search for Iraq's Weapons of Mass Destruction: Inspection, Verification, and Non-Proliferation* (New York: Palgrave MacMillan, 2005), 54.

271. Cordesman, *Iraq and the War of Sanctions*, 219–24.

272. In 1997, approximately 4,000 U.S. soldiers participated in this exercise under the Third Army's command and control. Haworth, *DAHSUM, FY 1998*, 52. A 1997 Third Army report called BRIGHT STAR "the largest OCONUS [outside the continental United States] exercise in which the U.S. Army participates." Annual Historical Review, Third U.S. Army, FY 1997, 6 Oct 1998, 23.

273. Douglas Jehl, "Attack on Tourist Bus Kills 9 Germans," *New York Times*, 19 Sep 1997, https://www.nytimes.com/1997/09/19/world/attack-on-cairo-tourist-bus-kills-9-germans-and-driver.html.

274. A similar scenario, in which the same large-scale training exercise overlapped with a

On 16 October 1997, the situation in Iraq escalated when Saddam threatened to end all cooperation with UNSCOM. Despite this warning, the UN Security Council split on the proposed travel restrictions. A compromise resulted in a new resolution that condemned Iraqi interference with UNSCOM efforts and "especially Iraqi actions endangering the safety of Special Commission personnel, the removal and destruction of documents of interest to the Special Commission and interference with the freedom of movement of Special Commission personnel."[275] It gave Iraq six months to comply with UN resolutions before travel restrictions would go into effect against "all Iraqi officials and members of the Iraqi armed forces who are responsible for or participate in instances of noncompliance."[276] Unlike previous resolutions on Iraq, this one was passed without unanimous consensus. Ten Security Council members voted yes but five abstained, including Russia, France, and China.[277]

Saddam sought to exploit the split in the Security Council. On 29 October, Iraq demanded all Americans be removed from the inspection teams and leave the country within seven days. Ten of the forty UNSCOM inspectors and 10 percent of the one hundred total UNSCOM employees in Baghdad were Americans, and the Iraqis claimed that the U.S. inspectors were spies. The sharing of intelligence between the United States and UNSCOM—much of it distilled from imagery taken on U–2 flights—made Saddam's shell game of moving and hiding WMD-related assets more difficult. It also formed the basis of Iraqi accusations that the U.S. inspectors were spying on Iraq's critical national infrastructure. However, intelligence-sharing was the only practical way to verify Iraq's compliance with UN resolutions. Because the UN lacked its own intelligence assets, it relied on member states to provide intelligence to aid inspections. On 2 November, Iraq threatened to shoot down U–2 aircraft conducting reconnaissance flights. Eleven days later, Iraq expelled U.S. inspectors, and Butler withdrew most of the other inspectors the following day.[278]

---

contingency operation, would arise after the September 11th attacks, when the Third Army headquarters first deployed to Egypt in October to oversee BRIGHT STAR, then shifted from Egypt to Kuwait the following month for Operation ENDURING FREEDOM. John A. Bonin, *U.S. Army Forces Central Command in Afghanistan and the Arabian Gulf During Operation ENDURING FREEDOM: 11 September 2001–11 March 2003*, monograph 1–03 (Carlisle, PA: Army Heritage Center Foundation, 2003), 41–43; Edmund J. Degen and Mark J. Reardon, *Modern War in an Ancient Land: The United States Army in Afghanistan, 2001–2014*, vol. 1 (Washington, DC: U.S. Army Center of Military History, [2021]), 65.
275. UN Security Council, Resolution 1134, The Situation Between Iraqi and Kuwait, S/RES/1134, 23 Oct 1997, http://unscr.com/en/resolutions/doc/1134.
276. S/RES/1134.
277. Pearson, *Search for Iraq's Weapons of Mass Destruction*, 68, table 3.7. Although troubling at the time, the division proved temporary. Four resolutions concerning Iraq over the following year passed with unanimous votes.
278. Alfred B. Prados, *Iraqi Challenges and U.S. Responses: March 1991 through October 2002*, RL31641 (Washington, DC: Congressional Research Service, 20 Nov 2002), 13.

Iraq's expulsion of UNSCOM's U.S. inspectors prompted a coalition military response. In October 1997, CENTCOM launched Operation DESERT THUNDER, which lasted until December 1998.[279] Its objectives were "to secure the full, free and unfettered access of UNSCOM weapons inspectors to suspected Iraqi WMD sites, to degrade near-term Iraqi flight operations, and to neutralize Iraqi surface-to-air missile (SAM) and selected parts of the Iraqi integrated air defense system (IADS)."[280] CENTCOM prepared, but never executed, strike packages of increasing duration and severity, labeled DESERT THUNDER I, DESERT THUNDER II, and DESERT THUNDER III.[281] As in previous crises, the United States deployed a second aircraft carrier to join the one already in the Persian Gulf and began enhancing its land-based air assets, bringing the total number of aircraft in the region to nearly 250. Great Britain prepared additional RAF aircraft and one aircraft carrier for deployment to the region.

Operation DESERT THUNDER soon brought results. The Russian foreign minister, Yevgeny M. Primakov, convinced Iraq on 20 November to readmit UN inspectors, including Americans, in exchange for a renewed promise that Russia would work toward a more balanced national representation on the inspection teams and the speedy lifting of sanctions. This agreement averted military action. An UNSCOM inspection team, including six inspectors from the United States, returned to Iraq the following day.

During DESERT THUNDER, as in previous crises with Iraq, the Third Army headquarters lacked the staff it needed to meet its mission to deploy and establish multiple forward command and control nodes. The headquarters at Fort McPherson not only maintained small forward support elements in Saudi Arabia, Kuwait, and Qatar, it also supplied a majority of the staff for ad hoc joint task forces that it activated during contingencies.[282] Responding to the pressing need for additional personnel, the Army authorized an increase of approximately 200 active duty positions for the Third Army staff. The additional personnel allowed the headquarters "to meet expanding mission requirements as an Army service component command."[283] The fact that Army leadership approved the change during a period of shrinking budgets and declining troop levels indicated the importance of the ARCENT missions.

---

279. William S. Cohen, Sec Def, *U.S. Military Involvement in Major Small-Scale Contingencies Since the Persian Gulf War*, Rpt to Cong., Mar 1999, 6.

280. Cohen, *U.S. Military Involvement in Major Small-Scale Contingencies*, Mar 1999, 6.

281. Knights, *Cradle of Conflict*, 178–80. Some Army sources use DESERT THUNDER I and DESERT THUNDER II to designate different parts of the operation, not strike packages. For example, see Tommy R. Franks, "Third Army: Ready to Respond and Regionally Engaged," *ARMY Magazine* 49, no. 10 (Oct 1999): 196.

282. In 1997, the assigned personnel at each headquarters were as follows: ARCENT–Kuwait (118), ARCENT–Saudi Arabia (59), and ARCENT–Qatar (19). Annual Historical Review, Third U.S. Army, FY 1997, 6 Oct 1998, 12–13.

283. Tommy R. Franks, "Third U.S. Army: 'One Team, One Fight, One Future,' Is a Reality," *ARMY Magazine* 48, no. 10 (Oct 1998): 181.

Events the following year would validate this decision, as Iraq continued to stonewall on weapons inspections. Iraq continued to bar UN inspectors from eight "sensitive" sites, including presidential palaces. The claim that these were purely private residences of the Iraqi leader rang hollow. One of Saddam's palaces encompassed more than 2,600 acres in Baghdad. (By comparison, the White House complex in Washington covers roughly eighteen acres.) Referring to the disputed Iraqi presidential sites, Clinton remarked, "We're not talking about a few rooms here with delicate personal matters involved."[284] He continued, "It is obvious that there is an attempt here, based on the whole history of this operation since 1991, to protect whatever remains of [Saddam's] capacity to produce weapons of mass destruction, the missiles to deliver them, and the feedstocks necessary to produce them."[285] UN Secretary General Kofi A. Annan traveled to Baghdad to convince Saddam to give "full, free, unfettered access to all suspected sites anywhere in Iraq," which Iraq had previously agreed to do.[286] In the midst of the crisis, the UN Security Council extended the oil-for-food program another six months, even though Iraq had refused to pump oil for three months and blamed the UN and the United States for disruptions in the flow of food and medicine.[287]

As tensions over inspections escalated, General Zinni, now the CINCCENT, requested a robust force. In response, more than 35,000 soldiers, sailors, airmen, and marines, as well as coalition forces deployed to the Gulf.[288] The Air Force sent additional bombers and strike aircraft to the region, and the Navy's USS *Guam* Amphibious Ready Group diverted from the Mediterranean Sea, bringing the 24th Marine Expeditionary Unit into the Gulf. Approximately 200 marines aboard USS *Ashland* disembarked in Kuwait City with tanks, light armored vehicles, and howitzers. They conducted live-fire exercises on the Udari Range complex for three days, 26–28 February.[289] The Army deployed a reinforced heavy battalion to Kuwait from Fort Stewart, Georgia. The 3d Battalion, 69th Armor, augmented the 1st Battalion, 30th Infantry, from Fort Benning, Georgia, which was already in Kuwait for INTRINSIC ACTION 98–1. The Army Reserve provided a critical capability by sending the 310th Chemical

284. William J. Clinton, *Public Papers of the Presidents of the United States: William J. Clinton, 1998, Book 1* (Washington, DC: Government Printing Office, 1998), 233.
285. Clinton, *Public Papers of the Presidents of the United States: William J. Clinton, 1998, Book 1*, 233.
286. Clinton, *Public Papers of the Presidents of the United States: William J. Clinton, 1998, Book 1*, 245.
287. UN Security Council, Resolution 1153, The Situation Between Iraq and Kuwait, S/RES/1153, 20 Feb 1998, http://unscr.com/en/resolutions/doc/1153. Compare to Clinton, *Public Papers of the Presidents of the United States: William J. Clinton, 1998, Book 1*, 505.
288. Tommy R. Franks, "Introduction," *Operation Desert Thunder–Kuwait, Tactics, Techniques, and Procedures*, CALL Newsletter, no. 00–6 (Mar 2000): 1. Compare to Clancy, Zinni, and Koltz, *Battle Ready*, 9.
289. Cmd Chronology, 3d Bn, 6th Marines, 1 Jul 1998, sec. 1, 8, and sec. 2, 2, Marine Corps History Div, Quantico, VA. (Note: sec. 1, 8 is misnumbered as sec. 2, 8.)

Company (Biological Integrated Detection System) with 192 soldiers.[290] The 32d Army Air and Missile Defense Command, functioning provisionally as a multicomponent unit with both active and reserve personnel, deployed with ninety-two soldiers and assumed command of two Patriot missile task forces: Task Force 1–1, formed from 1st Battalion, 1st Air Defense Artillery, already in Saudi Arabia as part of continuing Patriot rotations, and Task Force 3–43, made from 3d Battalion, 43d Air Defense Artillery, newly arrived in Kuwait for Operation DESERT THUNDER.[291] National Guard units protected the Patriot missile batteries as part of an ongoing mission, Operation DESERT SPRING.[292]

Soldiers from Fort Stewart, Georgia, arrive at Kuwait International Airport in support of Operation DESERT THUNDER.

(National Archives)

---

290. Haworth, *DAHSUM, FY 1998*, 74–75.

291. Rpt, n.d., sub: 32d Army Air and Missile Defense Command (AAMDC): The Desert Thunder Experience, 6–7, Historians Files, CMH. Since December 1996, the 32d AAMDC had been functioning provisionally as a multicomponent unit until a Modification Table of Organization and Equipment change made the new structure official on 16 October 1998. The initial deployment of active duty personnel to Kuwait took place in February. After President Clinton signed an executive order for a presidential selected reserve call-up on 24 February, ten reserve component soldiers of the Florida Army National Guard's 164th Air Defense Artillery Brigade were mobilized then deployed to Kuwait on 28 March 1998. Eight civilian contractors also deployed in support of the 32d AAMDC. Ibid., 2–3, 6–7. An additional seventeen Florida Army National Guard soldiers, led by Brig. Gen. Jerry L. Neff, deployed to Kuwait in Support of Operation DESERT THUNDER from 28 April to 20 May 1998. Memo, Capt. Kimberly A. Bodoh, HQ Commandant, Detachment 1, 32d Army Air and Missile Def Cmd, Florida Army National Guard, 30 Jun 2000, sub: Award of the Army Reserve Component Overseas Training Ribbon, Historians Files, CMH. For the Patriot missile battalions that deployed to Kuwait, see also Kirkpatrick, *"Ruck It Up!,"* 348, table 9.

292. Timothy E. Orr, "Small-Scale Contingency Operations and the Army National Guard," (Unpublished paper, Carlisle, PA: U.S. Army War College, 2003), 11. See also

These forces fell under the new Coalition Task Force–Kuwait (CTF-Kuwait), which the Third Army/ARCENT, now under Lt. Gen. Tommy R. Franks, established specifically for this operation to provide command and control for coalition land operations in theater.[293] The origins of this new ad hoc unit lay in a five-day terrain walk of the war plans in Kuwait involving more than fifty ARCENT commanders and staff. At this time, "reports indicated unusual and potentially threatening events by the Iraqis."[294] Saddam's threats to shoot down U.S. aircraft and expel weapons inspectors no doubt formed the content of this otherwise unspecified intelligence.

The reports caused the ARCENT staff to extend their stay in Kuwait to three weeks in order to conduct an extensive review of plans, which led to the development of CTF-Kuwait.[295] Although established by ARCENT, CTF-Kuwait reported directly to CENTCOM, which maintained operational control (*Figure 1*). The Third Army headquarters in Georgia provided administrative support to the new joint task force. General Zinni intended CTF-Kuwait (later called Joint Task Force–Kuwait then Combined Joint Task Force–Kuwait) to become his Joint Forces Land Component Command in case of war with Iraq, so he kept it active beyond the immediate crisis.[296] In maintaining a task force that could be expanded to establish a land component command at short notice, Zinni's approach represented a significant shift from the Gulf War model in which the CINCCENT functioned as the overall commander of ground forces. This new model gave the combatant commander the flexibility to delegate authority as needed, and helped to prevent the problems caused by the overcentralization of power seen during the Gulf War.[297]

Hines, "From Desert One to Southern Watch," 48.

293. Franks, "Third U.S. Army: 'One Team, One Fight, One Future,' Is a Reality," 178–79. Compare to Franks, "Third Army: Ready to Respond and Regionally Engaged," 194.

294. Annual Historical Review, Third U.S. Army, FY 1997, 6 Oct 1998, 1.

295. Annual Historical Review, Third U.S. Army, FY 1997, 6 Oct 1998, 1.

296. Lt. Gen. Anthony C. Zinni recalled, "But I also wanted the Army and Marine Corps to establish a forward element for the Joint Forces Land Component Command (JFLCC), which would run the coordinated ground battle in Kuwait. As a result, we established Joint Task Force (JTF) Kuwait." Clancy, Zinni, and Koltz, *Battle Ready*, 315. After Operation DESERT THUNDER, the CTF-Kuwait staff remained small and brigadier generals rotated through for thirty days at a time to command the task force. What ultimately became known as Combined Joint Task Force–Kuwait never fulfilled its purpose of becoming the land forces headquarters for war with Iraq. Because war came first in Afghanistan in 2001, CENTCOM designated the Third Army/ARCENT as a Coalition Forces Land Component Command apart from Combined Joint Task Force–Kuwait in November 2001, and the Coalition Forces Land Component Command absorbed Combined Joint Task Force–Kuwait at the beginning of the Iraq War in 2003.

297. At his retirement, General Zinni stated, "We can make the land component command arrangement work. There will be no more occasions in the Central Command's area of operations where Marines . . . fight one ground war and the Army fights a different ground war. There will be one ground war and a single land component commander." Quoted in Bonin, "Unified and Joint Land Operations," 7.

CENTCOM
U.S. Central Command

SOCCENT
Special Operations Command Central

CENTAF
U.S. Air Forces Central Command

ARCENT
U.S. Army Central Command

MARCENT
U.S. Marine Corps Forces Central Command

NAVCENT
U.S. Naval Forces Central Command

JTF SWA
Joint Task Force Southwest Asia

CTF-Kuwait
Coalition Task Force–Kuwait

ARCENT-KU
U.S. Army Central Command–Kuwait

ARCENT-SA
U.S. Army Central Command–Saudi Arabia

ARCENT-Q
U.S. Army Central Command–Qatar

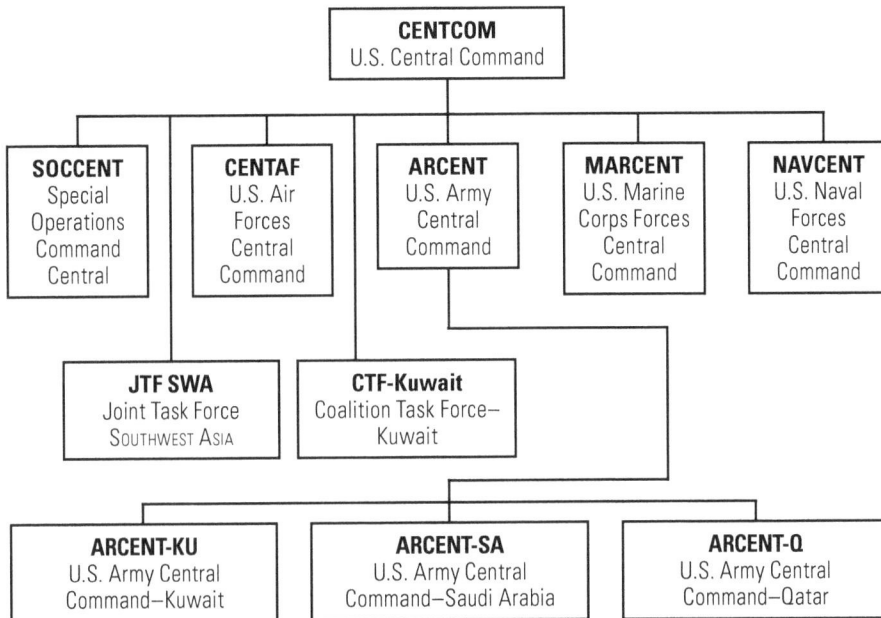

Figure 1. U.S. Central Command During Operations Desert Thunder and Desert Fox, 1997–1998

The standoff with Iraq ended on 23 February 1998 when Secretary General Annan struck a deal with Iraq over inspections at sensitive sites. The Secretary General agreed to appoint diplomats to accompany UNSCOM and IAEA inspectors. The following day, Annan confirmed that the build-up of coalition forces had helped win concessions from Iraq: "By demonstrating firmness and by making military force available were it to be needed, they contributed to the solution."[298] On 2 March, the UN Security Council passed a resolution, commending the Secretary General for securing a new agreement and warning that "any violations [of the agreement or other pertinent resolutions] would have [the] severest consequences for Iraq."[299]

Over the next few months, Iraq did not hinder UN inspections. Between 26 March and 3 April 1998, inspectors visited eight sensitive sites. Although they found no WMD or other prohibited material, they discovered evidence of extensive evacuations.[300] The U.S.-led coalition kept its forces on alert. In June, Clinton reported to congressional leaders that Iraq was providing access to UN inspectors in accordance with the 23 February agreement; however, the president thought it prudent "to

---

298. Quoted in "Annan Praises Britain and the United States," BBC News, 24 Feb 1994, http://news.bbc.co.uk/2/hi/events/crisis_in_the_gulf/59728.stm.
299. UN Security Council, Resolution 1154, The Situation Between Iraq and Kuwait, S/RES/1154, 2 Mar 1998, http://unscr.com/en/resolutions/doc/1154.
300. Prados, *Iraqi Challenges and U.S. Responses*, 15.

retain a significant force presence in the region to deter Iraq."[301] A larger-than-normal force remained in the Gulf, including two carrier battle groups, twice the pre-crisis number of cruise missiles, a heavy Army task force, and a Marine expeditionary unit. The 2d Battalion, 7th Cavalry, 1st Cavalry Division, which had deployed in May for INTRINSIC ACTION, formed the core of the Army task force in Kuwait. In addition to the U.S. military units, twenty nations either deployed forces to the region or were prepared to do so.

The conflict over inspections heated up again after Iraq once again suspended cooperation with UN inspections on 5 August, permitting only the ongoing monitoring of sites with previously installed surveillance equipment. By this point, the Clinton administration had tired of Saddam's cheat-and-retreat tactics, which not only interrupted weapons inspections but also prompted seemingly endless rounds of costly military build-ups to force the Iraqis to comply with UN resolutions. The thinking in Washington was shifting: instead of using force as a coercive tool, they would now use force as a means to degrade and damage Saddam's WMD capabilities, rather than relying on the inspections to thwart those capabilities.[302]

While the United States considered its next steps against Iraq, it struck a blow against terrorism. On 20 August, CENTCOM launched missile strikes against Afghanistan and Sudan as retaliation for the bombings of the U.S. embassies in Kenya and Tanzania two weeks prior by Osama bin Laden's al-Qaeda terrorist network. This organization claimed that the attacks, which killed 252 people, including 12 Americans, and wounded more than 5,000, were retaliation for the ongoing presence of U.S. troops in Saudi Arabia, home to Islam's most sacred sites. The brazen embassy bombings represented an increasing threat from nonstate actors in the region.

The split in the UN Security Council over the lifting of sanctions against Iraq widened in October. Russia, France, and China favored lifting the economic prohibitions if Iraq complied with all UN requirements regarding weapons of mass destruction. The United States, however, insisted on several additional criteria, such as returning Kuwaiti property, accounting for missing Kuwaiti prisoners, and compensating Kuwait for environmental damage.[303] On 31 October, frustrated by the impasse, Iraq suspended all cooperation with UN arms inspectors until the Security Council reviewed sanctions imposed in the wake of the Persian Gulf War and purged inspection teams of "American spies and agents."[304]

---

301. Clinton, *Public Papers of the Presidents of the United States: William J. Clinton, 1998, Book 1*, 502.
302. Knights, *Cradle of Conflict*, 183–84.
303. Cordesman, *Iraq and the War of Sanctions*, 349–50.
304. David Allen, "Kadena Jet Fighters Deploy to the Gulf Region," *Pacific Stars and Stripes*, 4 Nov 1998.

On the same day, the U.S. Congress passed the Iraq Liberation Act (ILA), which stated, "It should be the policy of the United States to support efforts to remove the regime headed by Saddam Hussein from power in Iraq and to promote the emergence of a democratic government to replace that regime."[305] The act did not authorize U.S. military intervention. American leaders hoped that the Iraqi people themselves would overthrow Saddam, a desire that dated back to the Iraqi invasion of Kuwait in 1990. After the successful conclusion of the Gulf War, President George H. W. Bush had voiced his support for removing Saddam Hussein from power, and his successor, Bill Clinton, used a covert CIA operation from 1994 to 1996 to assist Iraqi efforts at regime change. The ILA went further by officially advocating regime change and appropriating $97 million for various Iraqi opposition groups. Although Clinton signed the ILA into law, he had no intention of funding what he saw as unreliable Iraqi opposition groups that might start an insurgency inside Iraq, making the situation worse than the status quo.[306] Consequently, the United States spent few of these appropriated funds until 2001.[307] In the end, the ILA illustrated the policy-strategy mismatch within the Clinton administration. U.S. public policy supported removal of the Baathist regime in Baghdad, but the national strategy remained one of containment until conditions became ideal for regime change.

Two concerns drove the Clinton administration's caution: the unreliability of Iraqi opposition groups and the possibility that removing Saddam might destabilize both Iraq and the entire Middle East. Testifying before the Senate Committee on Armed Services, General Zinni explained that a contained Saddam was preferable to a fragmented post-Saddam Iraq or another failed state like Somalia or Afghanistan. Concerning Iraq, Zinni concluded, "It is possible to create a situation that could be worse."[308]

Short of pursuing regime change, the United States had options for punishing Iraq's ongoing noncompliance with U.N. resolutions. In November 1998, CENTCOM prepared another limited strike, Operation DESERT VIPER. President Clinton gave the "go" order after Butler, tired of Iraqi intransigence, evacuated all UN weapons inspectors from Baghdad on 11 November. However, the following day, Clinton called off the strike at the last minute when Iraq announced, yet again, that it would cooperate with UNSCOM and IAEA inspections without conditions.[309] The timing of the announcement, so close to the

305. *An Act to Establish a Program to Support a Transition to Democracy in Iraq*, PL 105–338, 105th Cong., 31 Oct 1998.
306. Michael R. Gordon and Bernard E. Trainor, *Cobra II: The Inside Story of the Invasion and Occupation of Iraq* (New York: Vintage, 2006), 14.
307. Marr, *Modern History of Iraq*, 254.
308. Testimony, Gen. Anthony C. Zinni, *Hearing on U.S. Policy on Iraq Before the Senate Committee on Armed Services*, 106th Cong. (28 Jan 1999), 27–28, Historians Files, CMH.
309. William J. Clinton, *Public Papers of the Presidents of the United States: William J. Clinton, 1998, Book 2* (Washington, DC: Government Printing Office, 1998), 2035. Compare

launch of an attack, suggested that Saddam was able to anticipate U.S. military action.[310] His sophisticated network of spies and informants apparently had detected the movement of U.S. forces. Iraq's promise to comply with UN inspections motivated CENTCOM to end Operation Desert Thunder, even though few in Washington believed Iraq would cooperate fully with the inspections regime.[311]

The Army played an important deterrence role in the operation. By 1997, Kuwait had agreed to allow (and fund) a "near-continuous presence" of U.S. ground combat troops in the country in the form of longer Intrinsic Action rotations, now typically lasting for four months, with few gaps between exercises.[312] This increased forward presence—one of the five pillars of General Peay's theater strategy— was not limited to the Army.[313] CENTCOM historian Jay E. Hines explained, "Comprised of Joint Task Force Southwest Asia as well as personnel from every service, including special operations, near-continuous presence promoted stability, deterred aggression, and facilitated peace-to-war transition."[314] When the threat level increased, as it did in February 1998, the Army augmented its battalion task force in Kuwait with additional forces. The ongoing presence of Army ground combat units signaled the United States' commitment to deter Iraqi aggression, defend Kuwait and

General Zinni as a lieutenant general
(Department of Defense)

to Knights, *Cradle of Conflict*, 197–200; Clancy, Zinni, and Koltz, *Battle Ready*, 1–3, 15.
310. Clancy, Zinni, and Koltz, *Battle Ready*, 16.
311. Cohen, *U.S. Military Involvement in Major Small-Scale Contingencies*, Mar 1999, 6. (Citation refers only to the first half of the sentence.)
312. End of Tour Rpt, Peay, 3 Nov 1997, 11. For the length of Intrinsic Action exercises, see Franks, "Third U.S. Army: 'One Team, One Fight, One Future,' is a Reality," 181. The term "near-continuous presence" was a phrase coined by the CENTCOM CJ-3 operations officer, Air Force Maj. Gen. Joseph E. Hurd, denoting an enhanced forward presence in the Gulf region. In practical terms, it meant keeping a carrier battle group in the Persian Gulf and a heavy battalion task force in Kuwait with little or no gaps in coverage. Telecon, J. Travis Moger, CMH, with General J. H. Binford Peay III, 3 Jul 2019.
313. Strategic plan, U.S. Central Command, *Shaping U.S. Central Command for the 21st Century*, 1995–1997, 8.
314. Hines, "From Desert One to Southern Watch," 47.

Self-propelled 155-mm. howitzers in Kuwait during Operation Desert Thunder
(ARMY Magazine)

Saudi Arabia, and secure vital U.S. interests in the region, especially the free flow of oil. However, a forward-deployed Army deterrence force alone could neither remove the threat of WMD nor make Iraq comply with UN resolutions.

OPERATION DESERT FOX

From his headquarters in Tampa, General Zinni decided he needed a new approach toward Iraq. He had noticed a pattern. Iraq's resistance to UN inspections gave it time to hide sensitive materials from UNSCOM inspectors. In response, the U.S.-led coalition would build up its forces to prepare for a military response, then Iraq would back down to avoid an attack. To end this cheat-and-retreat cycle, Zinni and Chairman of the Joint Chiefs of Staff General H. Hugh Shelton decided to "out fox" Saddam, hence the name Operation DESERT FOX.[315] The plan was to strike Iraq using coalition forces already available in the Gulf in order not to tip off Saddam that military action was imminent.

Iraq's continued resistance to UNSCOM inspections provided the justification for U.S. attacks. Despite its promises, Iraq continued to withhold requested documents and restrict access to sensitive sites. In a 15 December report to the Security Council, Butler detailed how Iraq had not provided the full cooperation it had promised the previous month and had imposed new restrictions on the inspectors' work.[316] Close coordination between Butler and Clinton's national security adviser, Samuel Richard "Sandy" Berger—close enough to become controversial—allowed the safe withdrawal of UNSCOM personnel from Iraq before military operations commenced.[317] Four hours after the last inspectors deplaned in Bahrain, Zinni launched his surprise attack, which lasted from 16 to 19 December.

The timing of the operation aroused partisan suspicions in Washington that Clinton had ordered attacks on Iraq to distract from presidential impeachment proceedings then underway in the House of

---

315. Clancy, Zinni, and Koltz, *Battle Ready*, 16–17. The code name proved controversial, because it had belonged to German Field Marshal Erwin Rommel during World War II. Later, Zinni claimed that he did not intend the term as a reference to the famous Nazi commander.
316. Ltr, Richard W. Butler, to the UN Sec General, 15 Dec 1998, https://www.un.org/Depts/unscom/s98-1172.htm.
317. Scott Ritter, who served as an arms control inspector for the special commission, explained that "the Butler-Berger hand-in-glove relationship during [the] UNSCOM 258 [inspection] was too cozy. Prior coordination, daily Butler-to-Berger situation updates during the inspection, and a mutual review of Butler's report before its submission to the secretary general infringed on the Security Council's powers. The final insult came on December 16. In the middle of Butler's presentation of his report to the council, and without prior consultation, a four-day bombing campaign, Operation DESERT FOX, began." Scott Ritter, *Endgame: Solving the Iraq Crisis* (New York: Simon & Schuster, 1999), 196.

Representatives.[318] However, in his address to the nation on the first day of the operation, Clinton explained that the intention behind the timing of the attacks was twofold: it denied Saddam time to prepare for the attack and it avoided launching an attack during the Islamic holy month of Ramadan, which would begin the coming weekend.[319] When a reporter asked Secretary of Defense William S. Cohen, a former Republican senator, whether the looming impeachment vote played any part in the decision to carry out military action against Iraq, Cohen replied, "The only fact, from my point of view, and from the chairman's point of view or from anyone else's point of view was what is in the national security interest of the United States."[320] In answer to another reporter's question, Cohen said, "I am prepared to place 30 years of public service on the line to say the only factor that was important in this decision is what is in the American people's best interests. There were no other factors."[321]

Secretary of Defense Cohen briefs members of the press on the attack of selected targets in Iraq during Operation DESERT FOX.

(National Archives)

The mission of Operation DESERT FOX, the largest attack on Iraq since the end of the Persian Gulf War, was "to degrade Iraq's capacity to develop and deliver weapons of mass destruction (WMD) and to degrade its ability to threaten its neighbors."[322] Air Force, Navy, Marine Corps, and RAF pilots flew more than 600 sorties. Some 200 aircraft and 20 ships delivered more than 600 bombs and 400 cruise missiles to their targets.[323] These weapons targeted nearly one hundred sites, including lethal weapons production or storage facilities, *Republican*

---

318. Clinton, *Public Papers of the Presidents of the United States: William J. Clinton, 1998, Book 2*, 2185.

319. Clinton, *Public Papers of the Presidents of the United States: William J. Clinton, 1998, Book 2*, 2184.

320. William S. Cohen, *Public Statements of William S. Cohen Secretary of Defense, 1998*, vol. 4 (Washington, DC: Historical Office, Office of the Secretary of Defense, n.d.), 2383.

321. Cohen, *Public Statements of William S. Cohen Secretary of Defense, 1998*, vol. 4, 2384.

322. William J. Clinton, *Public Papers of the Presidents of the United States: William J. Clinton, 1999, Book 1* (Washington, DC: Government Printing Office, 2000), 291.

323. Clancy, Zinni, and Koltz, *Battle Ready*, 17; Paul K. White, *Crises After the Storm: An Appraisal of U.S. Air Operations in Iraq Since the Persian Gulf War* (Washington, DC.: Washington Institute for Near East Policy, 1999), 59–60.

Guard units and facilities, government command, control, and communications facilities—including the Baath Party headquarters and intelligence headquarters—air defense systems, air fields, and one oil refinery. Almost half were destroyed or severely damaged, about a third moderately damaged, and a quarter either lightly damaged or not hit.[324] Iraq's Deputy Prime Minister Tariq Aziz claimed that allied action killed 62 Iraqi military personnel, including 38 Republican Guards, and wounded another 180.[325] The real number of Iraqi soldiers killed in action may have been as high as 2,000, with several times that many injured.[326] The coalition reported no friendly casualties. Assessing that the mission had achieved its goals, Zinni ordered an end to the bombings just before the beginning of Ramadan.

As in previous crises, the U.S. Army increased its presence in the region to deter possible Iraqi aggression. At its height, the Combined Joint Task Force–Kuwait reached approximately 6,000 personnel.[327] The 3d Infantry Division headquarters and its 2d Brigade headquarters provided command and control for Army units. Already in Kuwait were more than 1,200 troops belonging to Task Force 4–64, built around 4th Battalion, 64th Armor.[328] This unit remained in the country through the end of the year, while Task Force 3–15, centered on 3d Battalion, 15th Infantry, deployed to Kuwait on 17 December, bringing some 1,400 more soldiers.[329] The XVIII Airborne Corps sent a multiple launch rocket system, and the Florida Army National Guard mobilized some eighty soldiers of Detachment 1, 32d Army Air and Missile Defense Command, to help defend against Iraqi Scud missiles.[330] However, the air and missile defense troops were still in the United States when the operation ended and their mobilization with it.[331] From the active component, the V Corps in Germany sent an air defense

324. Prados, *Iraqi Challenges and U.S. Responses*, 16.
325. Prados, *Iraqi Challenges and U.S. Responses*, 17.
326. Dana Priest and Bradley Graham, "Airstrikes Took a Toll on Saddam, U.S. Says," *Washington Post*, 9 Jan 1999.
327. Franks, "Third Army: Ready to Respond and Regionally Engaged," 196, 198. This source provides the order of battle for ground forces during Operation DESERT FOX.
328. Annual Div History, 1998, 3d Inf Div (Mech), 1999, 2-1, Annual History Rpt Collection, CMH.
329. Annual Div History, 1998, 3d Inf Div (Mech), 1999, 4-2–4-3. Third Battalion, 15th Infantry, was deploying as planned for INTRINSIC ACTION 99–01.
330. Scott Maxwell, "National Guard Members Still Bound for Gulf," *Orlando Sentinel*, 20 Dec 1998.
331. Associated Press, "For National Guard Unit, Holiday Will Wait," *Orlando Sentinel*, 20 Dec 1998; Mike Oliver, "Local Troops Get Wish—Head Back Home," *Orlando Sentinel*, 22 Dec 1998. On 16 October 1998, the 164th Air Defense Artillery Brigade, 32d AAMDC, became Detachment 1, 32d AAMDC. The unit reverted to its earlier designation on 1 October 2004. Press Release, Lt. Col. Ron Tittle, Florida National Guard Public Affairs Ofc, "Florida's Missile Defense Command Converts to 164th ADA Brigade," 11 Mar 2004, Historians Files, CMH. (Many thanks to Alison Simpson, Florida Army National Guard Historian, for providing these documents.)

task force to Israel.[332] The North Carolina National Guard contributed the 130th Aviation Task Force to the overall effort, and the Marine Corps sent its 31st Marine Expeditionary Unit. However, these "just in case" forces never made contact with the enemy.

In the immediate aftermath of DESERT FOX, Saddam focused on neutralizing potential domestic threats. He launched yet another purge of military officers suspected of disloyalty, this time among the regular army divisions in the south, who came through DESERT FOX unscathed. He even executed one division commander.[333] In 1999, Saddam replaced several of his senior military commanders, including the chief of the general staff of the army and the chief of the *Republican Guard*. He also likely ordered the assassination of the Shi'a leader Grand Ayatollah Mohammed Sadeq al-Sadr in February of that year.[334] Once an important Arab Shi'a counterweight to the Iranian regime of Ayatollah Khomeini during the Iran-Iraq War, al-Sadr had become an increasingly vocal critic of Iraq's Baathist government by the late 1990s.[335] Unknown assailants gunned down al-Sadr and two of his sons as they left Friday prayers in a mosque in the Shi'a holy city of An Najaf. The killing sparked a two-month-long antigovernment uprising by al-Sadr's followers. The state-sponsored purges and killings illustrate the depth of Saddam's fear after the DESERT FOX attacks.

The success of the U.S. missile strikes caused General Zinni to shift his focus to what a post-Saddam Iraq might mean for the United States and its allies. Reports from inside Iraq—from diplomatic missions and other friendly sources—indicated that the four-day bombing campaign had destabilized Saddam's regime.[336] According to one observer, "Saddam consolidated and repositioned his forces in a manner that led GEN[eral] Zinni to believe that Saddam's hold on power was tenuous."[337] Because intelligence had convinced the CENTCOM commander that the collapse of Saddam's regime was a distinct possibility, Zinni decided to study what would happen if the regime in Baghdad really were to fall.

Zinni was confident that a U.S.-led coalition could easily defeat Iraq, but he worried about the postwar scenario. Developed and refined since the end of the Gulf War, the war plan "called for in excess of 350,000 troops and three Corps-level ground organizations."[338] Zinni's executive

---

332. Kirkpatrick, *"Ruck It Up!,"* 463, 466–67.
333. Knights, *Cradle of Conflict*, 207; Priest and Graham, "Airstrikes Took a Toll on Saddam, U.S. Says."
334. Sadeq al-Sadr's son, Muqtada al-Sadr, would later rise to prominence in Iraq following the dismantling of Saddam Hussein's government in 2003.
335. Rayburn and Sobchak, *U.S. Army in the Iraq War*, 19.
336. Clancy, Zinni, and Koltz, *Battle Ready*, 18.
337. Kidder, "Iraq Planning," 3.
338. Richard L. Stouder, "Rumsfeld's War" (Unpublished article, 20 Dec 2004), 3, Historians Files, CMH. Speaking of the 1998 iteration of Iraq war plans, Col. Stephen D. Kidder says, "We held steady on 5.33 Divisions (4 heavy, 1 light, 1 ACR [armored cavalry regiment]), 2 Corps, and 1 MEF [Marine expeditionary force] since

officer at CENTCOM, Col. Roland J. Tiso Jr. later recalled that "General Zinni recognized the need for a large force in OPLAN [Operation Plan] 1003 not so much for the destruction of the Republican Guard, but for the occupation to follow."[339] However, an important question about postwar Iraq remained in Zinni's mind: "After we defeat [Saddam], who takes care of reconstruction and all the attendant problems?"[340]

Zinni tapped defense contractor Booz Allen Hamilton to conduct a secret war game in Washington, D.C., from 28 to 30 June 1999. The purpose of the exercise, called the Desert Crossing Seminar, was "to identify interagency issues and insights on how to manage change in a post-Saddam Iraq."[341] More than seventy experts from the Department of Defense, Department of State, National Security Council, CIA, and U.S. Agency for International Development participated. According to Zinni, they were all willing to help define the problem, but no one other than the Department of Defense took seriously the need to develop a workable plan. Participants predicted the potential for civil chaos in a post-Saddam Iraq.[342] The final report bleakly concluded that "U.S. involvement could last for at least 10 years."[343] As a result of the Desert Crossing Seminar, CENTCOM planners developed a branch plan, using DESERT CROSSING as the code name, to prepare a military response to a sudden collapse of the regime in Baghdad.

our analysis informed us that it would take much more force to occupy and tame Iraq in a post-hostility environment than it would to remove the regime." Kidder, "Iraq Planning," 2.

339. Memoir, Tiso, Nov 2019, 2. Operation Plan 1003 was the primary plan for war in Iraq. For more on the naming of CENTCOM war plans, see page 59, note 115.

340. Clancy, Zinni, and Koltz, *Battle Ready*, 19.

341. AAR, Desert Crossing Seminar, CENTCOM, 28–30 Jun 1999, https://nsarchive2.gwu.edu/NSAEBB/NSAEBB207/index.htm, National Security Archive, George Washington University, Washington, DC.

342. John Heilprin, "1999 War Games Foresaw Problems in Iraq," *Washington Post*, 5 Nov 2006, http://www.washingtonpost.com/wp-dyn/content/article/2006/11/04/AR2006110400577.html.

343. AAR, Desert Crossing Seminar, CENTCOM, 28–30 Jun 1999.

After Operation DESERT FOX, Saddam refused to readmit UNSCOM inspectors or respect the no-fly zones. Coalition aircraft continued to patrol the skies, and Iraqi air defense forces tried to shoot them down. Iraqi pilots made occasional incursions into the exclusion zones—and even beyond the southern no-fly zone into Saudi Arabia—retreating to safety when challenged. On two separate occasions in late December 1998, Iraq fired surface-to-air missiles at coalition aircraft patrolling the northern and southern no-fly zones. Two pairs of Iraqi MiG–25s penetrated the no-fly zones on 5 January 1999. For the first time since 1993, U.S. pilots fired air-to-air missiles at Iraqi aircraft. However, none of the six projectiles hit its mark. Iraqi tactics made their aircraft both difficult and tempting targets. Military analyst Michael A. Knights explains, "Iraq's shallow, high-speed aerial incursions were almost impossible to intercept."[344] Iraqi pilots seemed to be playing a dangerous cat-and-mouse game with their opponents. Notably, the Iraqis made repeated—but unsuccessful—attempts to lure coalition aircraft out of their patrols in the no-fly zones. The presence of surface-to-air missiles and antiaircraft artillery batteries defending the free-fly zone around Baghdad led pilots to conclude that the Iraqis were deliberately trying to down coalition planes. The threat was real enough that coalition pilots called these attempts "SAMbushes."[345]

While coalition aircraft patrolled the skies over Iraq, airpower also figured prominently in NATO efforts to eject Serbian forces from Kosovo, a province of Yugoslavia populated by 90 percent ethnic Albanians but historically significant to Serbs. As in Bosnia, the Serbs undertook a violent ethnic cleansing campaign against civilians, causing a new refugee crisis. To stop the bloodshed and support the ethnic Albanian separatist militia in Kosovo, the U.S. Army sent Task Force HAWK from Germany to Albania in support of ongoing NATO operations in neighboring Kosovo. The task force included an aviation brigade with AH−64 Apache attack helicopters and a brigade-sized ground element. Numerous difficulties moving, sustaining, and employing American warfighting units embarrassed the Army and caused a public relations disaster. By the time the Army task force finally arrived, a seventy-eight-day NATO air campaign against Serbia was underway, and the Army stayed on the sidelines. Thus, the Army's ability to deploy forces rapidly to the Persian

---

344. Knights, *Cradle of Conflict*, 212.
345. Knights, *Cradle of Conflict*, 211–13.

Gulf region—where the United States had built political and military relationships; secured access, basing, and overflight permissions; and stockpiled equipment—did not necessarily translate into the capability to intervene quickly in other locations. After Russia convinced Serbia to withdraw its forces from Kosovo, beginning in June 1999 some 7,000 U.S. ground troops patrolled one of five security sectors of the province.[346] By the end of the 1990s, with experience in Somalia, Haiti, the Balkans, and elsewhere, peacekeeping had become a familiar mission to the Army.[347]

Meanwhile, coalition efforts in Iraq focused on protecting friendly aircraft. To deal with the increasing Iraqi threat, Clinton's national security team, at General Zinni's request, expanded the rules of engagement to allow a broader targeting of Iraqi air defenses. However, concerns about mission creep and pilot safety in the south and host-nation concerns in the north caused commanders to keep important restrictions in place. In the south, retaliatory strikes were delayed at least one day after a provocation to allow planners time to vet the targets. This was true before and after the changes to the rules of engagement. Also, the secretary of defense had to approve targets such as airfields or anything inside the unrestricted zone between the 33rd and 36th parallels. In the north, retaliatory strikes took place during the same mission and could not be delayed because of the Turks' prohibition against offensive operations launched from their country. However, the new rules of engagement, approved by Turkey, allowed the United States to hit any part of the Iraqi air defenses when U.S. pilots were threatened or fired upon by any other part.[348]

Iraq continued to target coalition aircraft. On 9 March, Secretary Cohen told reporters, "Since the end of last year, Iraq has violated the no-fly zones more than 100 times; they have fired more than 20 surface-to-air missiles at coalition aircraft; and they continually fired antiaircraft guns and rockets in an effort to shoot down our planes. In response to Iraqi aggression, our aircraft have fired back in self-defense; and we will continue to target Iraq's air-attack network as long as it continues to threaten our planes."[349] Attacks on coalition aircraft and violations of the no-fly zones continued throughout 1999 and into 2000.

Despite Iraqi attacks, coalition aircraft losses remained minimal. On 13 September 2000, an Iraqi air defense spokesman claimed that Iraq had

346. Brown, *Kevlar Legions*, 156–57; Kirkpatrick, *"Ruck It Up!,"* 459–95; R. Cody Phillips, *Operation Joint Guardian: The U.S. Army in Kosovo* (Washington, DC: U.S. Army Center of Military History, 2007); Stewart, *American Military History*, vol. 2, 450–55.
347. For more on the military's peacekeeping role, see David Fitzgerald, "Warriors Who Don't Fight: The Post–Cold War United States Army and Debates over Peacekeeping Operations," *Journal of Military History* 85, no. 1 (Jan 2021): 163–90; Frank N. Schubert, *Other Than War: The American Military Experience and Operations in the Post–Cold War Decade* (Washington, DC: Joint History Office, Office of the Chairman of the Joint Chiefs of Staff, 2013), https://www.jcs.mil/Portals/36/Documents/History/Monographs/Other_Than_War.pdf.
348. Knights, *Cradle of Conflict*, 213–22.
349. William S. Cohen, *Public Statements of William S. Cohen Secretary of Defense, 1999*, vol. 1 (Washington, DC: Historical Office, Office of the Secretary of Defense, n.d.), 568.

shot down ten allied aircraft since 17 December 1998.[350] Allied officials maintained that the coalition had lost no manned aircraft to enemy action since the Gulf War.[351] Still, fears of losing a pilot over Iraq caused the Department of Defense to reduce the number of flights over Iraq and have pilots take fewer risks during the remaining months of the Clinton administration. Later, one Operation NORTHERN WATCH commander, Air Force Maj. Gen. Edward R. Ellis, remarked, "By 2000, our job was to make sure that no-one thrust a microphone in the president's or prime minister's face because of us, and to make sure that one of us didn't end up being dragged through the streets of Baghdad, alive or worse."[352] The danger to coalition pilots was demonstrated by the fate of some coalition unmanned aerial vehicles. Iraqi surface-to-air missiles downed two RQ–1 Predator drones in 2001, and an Iraqi MiG–25 shot down a Predator in December 2002.[353]

To better respond to Iraqi threats, CENTCOM repositioned its forces in its area of operations. One goal was to reduce the coalition presence in Saudi Arabia where it had become increasingly difficult to operate. The Kuwaiti government agreed to build a new, larger military facility, Camp Arifjan, south of the capital, while improvements went on at Camp Doha. The Army continued deploying battalions to Kuwait three times a year for INTRINSIC ACTION exercises, expanded its pre-positioned stocks in Qatar, and based several logistics supply vessels in Qatar to help with in-theater transportation requirements. Qatar offered to improve its Al Udeid Air Base to house the Coalition Air Operations Center, then located at Prince Sultan Air Base in Saudi Arabia. Eventually, Al Udeid would house both the air operations center and CENTCOM's forward headquarters. The United States also increased its ability to launch operations into western Iraq from Jordan by conducting annual bilateral military training exercises in the desert south of Amman.[354] These improvements resulted in a coalition force that was less dependent upon Saudi Arabia and better able to respond to contingencies in the Persian Gulf region.

International terrorism proved to be a more immediate and serious threat to U.S. forces in the region than that posed by the situation in Iraq. On 12 October 2000, two al-Qaeda suicide bombers in a small explosives-laden boat blew a 40-by-60-foot hole in the guided-missile destroyer USS *Cole* as it was refueling at a port in Yemen, killing seventeen sailors and injuring thirty-nine. It was the costliest attack on a U.S. vessel since the USS *Stark* incident in 1987.

---

350. Prados, *Iraqi Challenges and U.S. Responses*, 17.
351. Prados, *Iraqi Challenges and U.S. Responses*, 17. Compare to Clancy, Zinni, and Koltz, *Battle Ready*, 18. It is unclear whether Iraq had shot down any unmanned coalition aircraft by this point.
352. Quoted in Knights, *Cradle of Conflict*, 230. The mission of Operation NORTHERN WATCH focused on enforcement of Iraq's northern no-fly zone, which had begun under Operation PROVIDE COMFORT.
353. Knights, *Cradle of Conflict*, 242.
354. Kidder, "Iraq Planning," 3.

Changes in leadership at the combatant command level and in the White House led the United States to become more hostile toward Iraq. In June 2000, Lt. Gen. Paul T. Mikolashek succeeded Franks as the commanding general of the Third Army; the following month, General Tommy R. Franks, promoted to four-star general, moved up to become the CENTCOM commander. President George W. Bush, who took office the following January, preferred a more aggressive approach to Iraq than his predecessor. A month after Bush's inauguration, U.S. and British combat aircraft struck five Iraqi air defense sites. Four of the five sites were in the free-fly zone around Baghdad, including the central node for the new fiber-optic cable infrastructure the Chinese were installing to upgrade Iraqi air defenses. Coalition attack aircraft, firing from within the southern no-fly zone, used satellite-guided stand-off weapons to hit the targets above the 33rd parallel. Several of these "precision" glide bombs went astray, missing their mark. The attack took on heightened significance as the first belligerent act of a new president, whose father had led a multinational coalition to victory over Iraq almost exactly ten years before. Images of coalition aircraft bombing Baghdad, alight with antiaircraft fire, evoked memories of the Gulf War.[355]

Then, on 11 September 2001, tragedy struck the United States when nineteen terrorists hijacked commercial airliners and used them as weapons to carry out suicide attacks on the World Trade Center's twin towers in New

General Franks
(Department of Defense)

General Mikolashek as a brigadier general
(Department of Defense)

355. Knights, *Cradle of Conflict*, 236–38; Prados, *Iraqi Challenges and U.S. Responses*, 18.

York and the Pentagon in Washington, D.C.[356] The attacks killed nearly 3,000 people, the deadliest terrorist act in U.S. history. Although Saddam Hussein immediately denied involvement in the attacks, Iraq was the only Middle Eastern nation that did not send official condolences to the United States. Just nine hours before the first plane hit the World Trade Center, Iraq had shot down a U.S. Predator drone near Al Basrah. General Franks ordered a retaliatory strike.[357] As Knights points out, this meant that "the first U.S. military action after the September 11th attacks would not fall against the Taliban (Afghanistan's regime) but rather against Iraq air-defense operators."[358] Osama bin Laden, not Saddam Hussein, had been behind the attacks; and Afghanistan, not Iraq, had harbored Bin Laden and his al-Qaeda organization. However, in the wake of the worst attack on American soil since Pearl Harbor, many in the Bush administration tended to blur the two threats together. Fifteen days after September 11th, President Bush asked Defense Secretary Donald H. Rumsfeld to examine the war plans for Iraq. This request began a bureaucratic and military process that culminated in the Bush administration's decision to invade Iraq in March 2003.[359]

---

356. Passengers on one of the four hijacked airliners, United Flight 93, attacked the four terrorists in control of the vessel. Moments later, the aircraft crashed into the ground near Shanksville, Pennsylvania, twenty minutes' flying time from Washington, D.C., killing everyone aboard. National Commission on Terrorist Attacks Upon the United States, *The 9/11 Commission Report: Final Report of the National Commission on Terrorist Attacks Upon the United States*, authorized ed. (New York: W. W. Norton, n.d.), 10–14.
357. Tommy R. Franks, *American Soldier* (New York: Regan Books, 2004), 241.
358. Knights, *Cradle of Conflict*, 242.
359. Donald H. Rumsfeld, *Known and Unknown. A Memoir* (New York: Sentinel, 2011), 425.

Iraq remained a threat after the 1991 Persian Gulf War. Although a stunning victory for the U.S.-led coalition, this conflict neither removed Saddam Hussein from power nor eliminated Iraq's ability to threaten its neighbors. Saddam's brutal repression of internal uprisings illustrated the firmness of his grip on power. His military adventurism in October 1994 underscored both his ability and willingness to threaten Kuwait, whether or not he intended a second invasion. Neither assassination nor coup attempts—including those supported by the CIA—managed to dislodge Saddam and his Baathist regime. Thus, Iraq remained a potential menace in the Middle East. To contain Iraqi aggression and enforce UN sanctions, the United States intervened militarily in the region throughout the 1990s and beyond. Against this background, several important conclusions come into focus.

First, competing priorities and shrinking budgets put stress on the U.S. Army and undermined its ability to execute its missions. As the U.S. Congress pursued a post–Cold War peace dividend, Army budgets declined throughout the 1990s, hitting a low of $60.4 billion in 1998.[360] They began increasing in 2000, the last year of Bill Clinton's presidency.[361] The number of active duty Army divisions dropped from eighteen during Operation DESERT STORM in 1991 to ten in 1996. Active duty personnel strength fell annually until it reached 480,000 soldiers in 2001.[362] When the September 11th attacks took place, the Army was at its smallest size since 1940. Although Army budgets declined and troop levels shrank throughout the decade, the operational tempo remained high because of ongoing commitments in Germany, Korea, the Sinai Peninsula, and Kuwait, as well as new operations in Somalia, Haiti, Bosnia, Kosovo, and elsewhere. Army leaders called up reservists to alleviate the strain.[363] War plans for Iraq, developed in the 1990s, envisaged even greater roles for reserve forces in combat operations; however, questions about reserve readiness and the lack of sufficient support units caused experts to doubt

---

360. Haworth, *DAHSUM, FY 1998*, 19.
361. Haworth, *DAHSUM, FY 2000*, 12.
362. Koontz, *DAHSUM, FY 2001*, 12.
363. In a 1999 report to Congress, Secretary of Defense William S. Cohen observed, "Because of high OPTEMPO [operating tempo] and PERSTEMPO [personnel tempo] demands on the active component, reserve components are being called upon more frequently and for longer periods in peacetime than ever before." Cohen, *U.S. Military Involvement in Major Small-Scale Contingencies*, Mar 1999, 27.

the Army's ability to execute its contingency plans for a second regional war. Abetted by a fiscally conservative Congress, the same Clinton administration that had introduced the two-theater strategy undermined the military's ability to execute it.

Second, the Army turned its heavy brigades into a rapid deployment force for the Persian Gulf. One of the most important lessons the Army had learned during Operation DESERT SHIELD was the value of moving a large force overseas, especially ground combat units, as quickly as possible.[364] Now, whenever a crisis developed in Iraq, the Army could hurry heavy ground forces to Kuwait. There, the troops drew equipment and supplies from pre-positioned stockpiles, which made rapid deployment possible. Rushing to and operating in Kuwait and neighboring countries became routine. Not only did maneuver units and their support elements deploy, brigade, division, and even the ARCENT forward headquarters learned how to move rapidly and set up operations in Kuwait. Over the course of a decade, the Army—drawing on expertise developed from shifting forces to Europe in Cold War REFORGER exercises—built the capacity to move a heavy division to the Middle East in less than half the time it took in 1990.

Third, the Army improved its ability to fight in the desert. A robust and realistic training regimen, including combined-arms live-fire exercises, at the National Training Center in California, on the Udari Range complex in Kuwait, and in Egypt for BRIGHT STAR exercises built critical warfighting skills in a desert environment. Frequent deployments to the Middle East established and refined procedures for such movements and made travel to and operating in a hot, arid climate and rocky, sandy terrain familiar, if not routine. These recurring training exercises—supported by improved infrastructure at home and overseas—prepared the Army to deploy to and operate in a harsh desert environment.

Fourth, containing Iraq was expensive but not as expensive as conventional warfare. Before the terrorist attacks on 11 September 2001, U.S. government leaders and policy experts considered the risk of a full-scale ground war with Iraq too high a price for regime change. Moreover, Iraq provided a counterweight to Iran, America's former ally turned virulent adversary. Destabilization inside Iraq threatened the balance of power in the region. As long as the Iraqi threat was contained, the situation remained manageable, although recurring crises made this strategy frustrating and expensive. The United States spent approximately $7.5 billion on Iraqi containment and deterrence operations from the end of the Gulf War through the conclusion of the decade. (*See Appendix B, Table 1.*) This amount represented a fraction of the estimated $61 billion that it cost to remove the Iraqi Army from Kuwait in 1991 by conventional military force, although other nations paid all but $4.7 billion.[365]

---

364. DoD, *Conduct of the Persian Gulf War*, 10 Apr 1992, 59.
365. Stephen Daggett, *Costs of Major U.S. Wars*, RS22926 (Washington, DC: Congressional

Fifth, sanctions could do only so much to compel Saddam Hussein to comply with the 1991 cease-fire agreement. Whereas containment efforts focused primarily on preventing Iraq from attacking its neighbors, sanctions reduced Iraq's ability to acquire prohibited materiel and put pressure on Saddam Hussein to give up his nation's WMD programs. Although the IAEA effectively dismantled Iraq's nuclear program and UN inspectors dealt successfully with Iraq's biological and chemical weapons, doubts about WMD programs remained because of limited U.S. intelligence and Iraq's lack of full compliance with the inspections regime. Iraq's partial and grudging cooperation with inspections resulted from Saddam's competing goals of achieving sanctions relief while also appearing strong to his neighbors and the rest of the world. Even if Iraq no longer possessed stockpiles of WMD—and short of full Iraqi compliance there was no way to be sure—it retained the ability to restart its ballistic missile and WMD programs once the UN lifted sanctions, despite the best efforts of weapons inspectors. Only by removing Saddam from power by force in 2003 did the United States and its allies finally eliminate Iraq's nuclear ambitions and greatly reduce the possibility that it would arm terrorists with WMD or deploy them again against foreign and domestic adversaries as in the 1980–1988 Iran-Iraq War.

Sixth, before 2001 operational plans for war against Iraq were reactive in nature. The family of war plans developed in the 1990s assumed that an aggressive move by Saddam Hussein—such as *Republican Guard* units crossing into the no-drive zone—would trigger the plan. This assumption aligned with the longstanding U.S. aversion to preventative war. The tragedy of September 11th radically altered the calculus. In fact, President Bush introduced the possibility of preemption in his 2002 National Security Strategy.[366] Even before this shift in policy, U.S. presidents had used limited military action to coerce or punish nations. However, the idea that the United States might pursue a full-scale war without a clear military provocation was a significant change.[367]

Research Service, 24 Jul 2008), 2–3, 3nA. Estimates are incremental costs of operations, meaning the expenses of war-related activities over and above the regular, nonwartime costs for defense. They do not include veterans' benefits, interest on war-related debts, or assistance to allies.

366. George W. Bush, *The National Security Strategy of the United States of America* (Washington, DC.: The White House, Sep 2002), 6, 15–16, https://2009-2017.state.gov/documents/organization/63562.pdf.

367. On 16 October 2002, the U.S. Congress, in a bipartisan vote, ratified preemption by giving President Bush authorization to use military force against Iraq: "The President is authorized to use the Armed Forces of the United States as he determines to be necessary and appropriate in order to— (1) defend the national security of the United States against the continuing threat posed by Iraq; and (2) enforce all relevant United Nations Security Council resolutions regarding Iraq. *Authorization for Use of Military Force Against Iraq Resolution of 2002*, PL 107–243, 107th Cong., 16 Oct 2002, https://www.govinfo.gov/content/pkg/PLAW-107publ243/pdf/PLAW-107publ243.pdf.

Seventh, even before the September 11th attacks, U.S. presidents practiced unilateralism when they deemed it to be in the national interest. The United States worked within an international framework to contain Iraq but was willing to act independently. Numerous examples illustrate this inclination, including the creation of two no-fly zones without explicit UN mandates, executing Operations DESERT STRIKE in 1996 and DESERT FOX in 1998, and the 1995–1996 CIA mission in northern Iraq aimed at bringing about regime change. In 1998, President Clinton explained, "The United States does not relish moving alone because we live in a world that is increasingly interdependent. We'd like to be partners with other people. But sometimes we have to be prepared to move alone."[368] After September 11th, the U.S. news media and public opinion often characterized President George W. Bush's strategy with regard to Iraq as "go it alone," despite the international coalition he built for Operation IRAQI FREEDOM.[369] However, both Clinton and the elder Bush took a unilateral approach toward Iraq when they determined it to be in the United States' national interest.

Eighth, despite the United States' willingness to act unilaterally on occasion, host nation access, basing, and overflight permissions proved crucial to military success. Conversely, a lack of support from partner nations complicated matters. Turkish antipathy toward the Kurds made operations in northern Iraq to support the Kurds difficult, because the nearest U.S. base was in Incirlik, Turkey. The absence of Saudi support for retaliation against Iraq for attacking Kurdish civilians in the fall of 1996, including the denial of bases in Saudi Arabia, created planning challenges for Operation DESERT STRIKE and forced the United States to opt for cruise missile attacks instead of more accurate and lethal air strikes. Increasing restrictions on the use of Saudi bases caused the United States to reposition its forces in the region, with Kuwait and Qatar accepting a larger U.S. military presence. In addition to friction among regional groups, long-term underlying problems complicated U.S.–host nation relations. Political, ethnic, and religious differences between the Muslim world and the West, plus unwavering U.S. support for Israel, frustrated Middle East diplomacy. All governments in this overwhelmingly Islamic part of the world remained sensitive to the risks associated with an ongoing U.S. military presence in the region, and radical groups such as al-Qaeda used this sensitivity to inflame Muslims and turn popular opinion against the United States and its allies.[370] In trying to solve one problem (Iraq),

368. Clinton, *Public Papers of the Presidents of the United States: William J. Clinton, 1998, Book 1,* 93.
369. Stephen A. Carney, *Allied Participation in Operation IRAQI FREEDOM* (Washington, DC: U.S. Army Center of Military History, 2011), 1.
370. For al-Qaeda leaders' opposition to the ongoing presence of U.S. troops in Saudi Arabia, see Lawrence Wright, *The Looming Tower: Al-Qaeda and the Road to 9/11* (New York: Alfred A. Knopf, 2006), 156–60, 169–70, 209–12, 259.

the United States and its allies unintentionally exacerbated another one (international terrorism).

Finally, international terrorism posed an increasing threat. Terrorists attacked the World Trade Center in New York in 1993, U.S. military facilities in Saudi Arabia in 1995 and 1996, two U.S. embassies in Africa in 1998, and the USS *Cole* in Yemen in 2000. The 2001 terrorist attacks by al-Qaeda in New York, Pennsylvania, and Washington killed more Americans than all of these previous incidents combined. The prospect of Iraq supplying terrorists with WMD—although unlikely based on past behavior—appeared a far greater and more plausible risk after September 11th. The second Bush administration deemed the strategy of Iraqi containment that had been in place since the end of the Gulf War no longer viable. After punishing the Taliban regime in Afghanistan for harboring the terrorist organization that had masterminded the September 11th attacks, the administration shifted its focus to effecting regime change and removing the threat posed by Saddam Hussein's Iraq.

George W. Bush addresses the United Nations General Assembly in New York City on the issues concerning Iraq, 12 September 2002.

(*National Archives*)

COMMANDERS LIST

CHAIRMEN OF THE JOINT CHIEFS OF STAFF	
General Colin L. Powell, USA	1989–1993
General John M. D. Shalikashvili, USA	1993–1997
General H. Hugh Shelton, USA	1997–2001
General Richard B. Myers, USAF	2001–2005

COMMANDERS OF THE UNITED STATES CENTRAL COMMAND	
General H. Norman Schwarzkopf Jr., USA	1988–1991
General Joseph P. Hoar, USMC	1991–1994
General J. H. Binford Peay III, USA	1994–1997
General Anthony C. Zinni, USMC	1997–2000
General Tommy R. Franks, USA	2000–2003

COMMANDERS OF THE THIRD UNITED STATES ARMY	
Lt. Gen. John J. Yeosock, USA	1989–1992
Lt. Gen. James R. Ellis, USA	1992–1994
Lt. Gen. Steven L. Arnold, USA	1994–1997
Lt. Gen. Tommy R. Franks, USA	1997–2000
Lt. Gen. Paul T. Mikolashek, USA	2000–2002

APPENDIX B

TABLE 1—INCREMENTAL COSTS OF DEPARTMENT OF DEFENSE CONTINGENCY
OPERATIONS AGAINST IRAQ, 1991–1999,[a]
(*MILLIONS OF DOLLARS*)

FISCAL YEAR[b]	OPERATION	TOTAL
1991–1993	UN Iraq–Kuwait Observer Mission/ UN Iraq Observer Mission	32.4
1991–1999	PROVIDE COMFORT/NORTHERN WATCH	1,336.9
1993–1999	SOUTHERN WATCH/AIR EXPEDITIONARY FORCE	5,528.6
1995	VIGILANT WARRIOR	257.7
1997–1999	DESERT STRIKE/INTRINSIC ACTION	246.7
1998	DESERT THUNDER	43.5
1999	DESERT FOX	92.9
1991-1999	TOTAL IRAQ	**7,538.7**

a. Incremental costs include the costs of contingency-related activities over and above normal operating expenses.
b. Fiscal year reflects billing years. Some operations continued beyond FY 1999.

Source: Nina M. Serafino, *Peacekeeping: Issues of U.S. Military Involvement*, IB94040 (Washington, DC: Congressional Research Service, 25 Aug 2000), 15.

ABBREVIATIONS

ACR	armored cavalry regiment
AMC	U.S. Army Materiel Command
ARCENT	U.S. Army Central Command
AWR	Army War Reserve
CENTCOM	U.S. Central Command
CIA	Central Intelligence Agency
CINCCENT	Commander in Chief of U.S. Central Command
CTF	coalition task force; combined task force
IAEA	International Atomic Energy Agency
JTF	joint task force
KDP	Kurdistan Democratic Party
MFO	multinational force and observers
MLRS	multiple launch rocket system
NATO	North Atlantic Treaty Organization
PACOM	U.S. Pacific Command
PUK	Patriotic Union of Kurdistan
RAF	Royal Air Force
SNA	Somali National Alliance
SWA	Southwest Asia
U.S.	United States
UN	United Nations
UNITAF	unified task force
UNOSOM	UN Operations in Somalia
UNSCOM	UN Special Commission
WMD	weapons of mass destruction

Additional Footnote Abbreviations

AAMDC	Army Air and Missile Defense Command
CMH	U.S. Army Center of Military History
Cong.	Congress
DAHSUM	*Department of the Army Historical Summary*
DoD	Department of Defense
FY	fiscal year
sess.	session
SO	special orders
sub	subject

THE AUTHOR

Jourden Travis Moger received his PhD in history from the University of California, Santa Barbara. A veteran of Operation Desert Thunder, discussed in this monograph, and Operation Iraqi Freedom, Moger is now a historian at the U.S. Army Center of Military History. He has published two articles about U.S.-led operations against Iraq in *Army History*.

www.ingramcontent.com/pod-product-compliance
Lightning Source LLC
Chambersburg PA
CBHW081422090426
42740CB00037B/3037